Changing the World Through Prayer

. . . an ADRA prayer journal

*"Behold, I am the LORD, the God of all flesh.
Is there anything too hard for Me?"*
Jeremiah 32:27

PUBLISHED BY WORD, INC.
DALLAS, TEXAS

ISBN: 0–8499–5176–3

Presented to:

_____

from

_____

date

_____

TABLE OF CONTENTS

FOREWORD

There were just the two of us sitting in the car in the middle of the parking lot, praying, all thoughts of lunch forgotten. It was the day that Ralph would have to give his answer. We prayed that both of us would be impressed of the right thing to do . . .

PAT: It was October 1985, and we were facing a very difficult decision. Ralph had been asked to become the president of the Adventist Development and Relief Agency (ADRA), whose Maryland headquarters were a continent away from our California home. We had a thousand reasons to say no. He had just moved his parents to California in April. Our youngest daughter was still living at home. Our son was moving from Wyoming to Sacramento, joining two other children already living on the West Coast.

If we accepted this call, we would have to leave our family behind. We would be "orphans."

RALPH: I felt a tremendous responsibility to say yes to this urgent request. I felt I had the qualifications they were looking for, having been in church administration for most of my adult life. Many years spent working overseas had given me a good perspective to bring into a situation like ADRA. Plus, I had been involved in ADRA-type projects in Korea and China.

But I was so happy with my work in Southern California. It was a great conference to work in, our constituents treated us like royalty, I was home every night . . .

"Are you sure you want to do this?" our friends asked. "This would be such a change."

The sun streamed through the windshield. We looked at each other, suddenly at peace. Yes. It was the right thing to do. No matter what God wanted us to do, it would be all right. We were within His will, and nothing was too hard for Him.

RALPH: During the next two years as I struggled with the problems of the newly reorganized agency, I sometimes asked, "Lord, what have I done? Why have you brought me here? Where are You in all this?" It was a very lonely time. But even though we couldn't see through the dark clouds, the bright future was there all the time. And with God's blessing, it began to shine through.

PAT: Memories crowded my mind that day in the parking lot, all the experiences the Lord had led Ralph and me through. He was with us during the fall of Saigon in 1975. Ralph, as president of the Vietnamese conference, directed the dramatic evacuation of all church national and overseas personnel as the North Vietnamese forces closed in on Saigon.

During those last months, Ralph had been called back to Vietnam every week or two. But this time when I took him to the airport in Singapore to catch his plane for Saigon I said, "You're not coming back at the usual time."

"I'll be back Wednesday," he insisted.

"No," I said, "you'll be staying to the end." I don't know why I knew, except that I believe God wanted to reassure me. Then every time word came back that his plane had been delayed, it wasn't frightening for me because I didn't expect him back.

Since all communication between Saigon and Singapore had been cut off, we didn't know what was happening in Saigon. Every day other women, whose husbands were also connected with the evacuation, got together with me for prayer. One day as I sat in the office typing, a terrible feeling came over me. Something was wrong. Quickly, I gathered everyone into the worship room for a season of prayer. We stayed there until the Lord gave me peace.

Then I received word that everyone was out except Ralph, but he was to leave in an hour and a half and would call me. When I didn't hear from him, the people at headquarters offered to try to reach him again. The peace was still there. "No, everything's okay," I said. And it was. God had promised. Nothing is too hard for Him. I went to bed and slept. Ralph called at 8:00 the next morning. He was out.

RALPH: Pat is a woman of prayer. Our kids say that if any of us make it into the kingdom it will be because of Pat's prayers.

Dear friend, this prayer journal is filled with steps to follow for Bible reading, meditation, and prayer. It carries you all the way through the New Testament with references from the Old Testament that apply. Your life will be richer and more abundant as you feel God's Spirit guiding and enhancing your life. To the extent that you give of your time, thought, and commitment to the enjoyment and use of this book, you will find peace, joy, and fulfillment far beyond your dreams. God bless you every day!

Ralph and Pat Watts

INTRODUCTION

The purpose of a *devotional prayer journal* is to provide a tool, a structured means, by which a Christian who loves and wants to serve the Lord Jesus Christ may be enabled on a daily basis to meet Him and have a complete worship experience. God the Father has created us to have fellowship with Himself. God the Son died and rose again to open the way for us to have fellowship with Him. God the Holy Spirit opens our minds and hearts to understand and respond to God's Word, the Bible, and intercedes for us with groanings that cannot be uttered whenever we pray (see Romans 8:26).

If God went to the lengths He did to make it possible for us to know Him and have fellowship with Him, it behooves us to do whatever it takes to realize God's purpose in creating and redeeming us. As Paul wrote to the Philippians:

"That I may know Him and the power of His resurrection, and the fellowship of His sufferings, being conformed to His death. . . ." (Philippians 3:10)

God plants this desire in the hearts of His children. How shall we respond? This devotional prayer journal suggests a way. It has a simple, logical format that incorporates all the important features of a complete time of devotions.

In order of priority, the journal contains the following elements:

1. *Bible Readings.* This journal takes the reader through the entire New Testament in a year. Related Old Testament readings are included for each day. Jesus personally prayed for us to have this experience (see John 17:20).

2. *Meditations.* Not only must we read God's inspired, inerrant Word, we must reflect on the truth of what we have read. One meditation per week, based on readings from that week, is also included (see Joshua 1:8).

3. *Memory Verses.* To secure the truth of the daily readings in our minds and hearts, a memory verse for each week is suggested. There is no substitute for hiding God's Word in

our hearts (see Psalm 119:11).

4. *Prayer Requests.* Space to write prayer requests and prayer results is provided. God wants us to bring everything to Him in prayer and to pray in accordance with His revealed will (see Philippians 4:6).

If we build these features into our devotional lives, we will be laying a foundation for powerful, godly living.

IMPORTANCE OF A DEVOTIONAL PRAYER JOURNAL

The way by which we as Christians receive *power* for daily living, and the means through which God releases His *grace* into the world, is believing *prayer*. As Christians, we are "the salt of the earth" and "the light of the world" (Matthew 5:13–14). We cannot give light to a dark world or be used by God as a preservative in a decadent society unless we are plugged into the *power* source, God Himself, through believing *prayer*.

Many times Christians in our society dash off quickie prayers as they fall asleep at night or just before they need God's help for some specific task. We have allowed ourselves to become anemic spiritually because we regard everything else in our hurry-up lives as more urgent and more important than our devotional time with the Lord.

What are we saying by this behavior? Are we telling God we are too busy to spend quality time with Him? Are we saying we do not *need* what He has provided in the way of spiritual resources, that we do not *need* to hear Him speak to us through His Word, or that we do not *need* to talk to Him in prayer? Surely, we would never consciously express such thoughts. Perhaps we should remind ourselves of the words of the Lord as He taught His disciples about their total dependence on Him:

> "I am the vine, you are the branches. He who abides in Me, and I in him, bears much fruit; for without Me you can do nothing."
> (John 15:5)

Notice the benefit of drawing from our *power* source, the Lord Jesus Christ: we become *very* fruitful in our work and witness for Christ!

To receive this benefit, we must make the time each day to spend alone with the Lord. When we want to accomplish a certain number of things in a given day, we write up a "to do" list and check it off when we have completed the things we want to get done. A *devotional prayer journal* serves a similar purpose, by outlining day by day and week by week a program of Bible reading, meditation, Scripture memorization, and prayer. If it is all laid out for us, we are less likely to forget our devotions or omit vital parts of our prayer life.

Because it is important for us to *respond* to what God is teaching us, and to have a permanent *record* of lessons and blessings, places are provided for the journal user to write down applications of Scripture and results of prayer. Paul indicated the prayers he was making on behalf of the churches to which he wrote near the beginning of most of his letters (see Romans 1:8–10). He did this to communicate both *care* and *encouragement*. When we record the results of our prayers, we are reminded of how much God *cares* for us. At the same time, we are *encouraged* to persevere in our worship of the Lord.

THE SPECIFIC MEANING OF PRAYER

Prayer is asking God persistently in faith for the right thing with the right motive. Let us reflect on this definition of prayer:

1. *Asking God.* Even though God knows what we need before we ask Him (see Matthew 6:8), He still bids us to ask (see Matthew 7:7). Prayer is a "declaration of dependence" on God, an acknowledgment that everything good in our lives is given to us by God (see James 1:17).

2. *Persistently.* On more than one occasion, Jesus taught His disciples that we are never to give up in bringing our needs to God (see Luke 11:5–8; 18:1–5). This is sometimes called importunate prayer. It means we are to keep on asking, seeking, and knocking until God answers (see Luke 11:9).

3. *In Faith.* Jesus also taught His disciples that if they ask God for something, they must believe He will answer. If they believe without doubting, they will receive what they ask for (see Matthew 21:21–22; Mark 11:23). James says that to do otherwise is to be like the waves tossed by the wind, to be double-minded (James 1:6–8).

4. *For the Right Thing.* The Lord's Prayer teaches us that it is always right to pray that God be glorified, that His will be done, that our real needs be met, and that we be kept from evil (see Matthew 6:9–13). Beyond these things, it is always right to pray for what God has revealed to be His will in the Bible (see 1 John 5:14–15), to believe that He will answer if we do His revealed will (see 1 John 3:22).

5. *With the Right Motive.* The right motive in prayer is to seek the honor and glory of the Lord Jesus Christ in what we ask (see John 12:28; 17:1). When our prayers are "gimme" prayers, when we seek to satisfy our own desires instead of God's, we know at the outset we will not receive what we ask for (see James 4:3).

As believers, we sometimes wonder if we are praying for the right thing with the right motive. If we have been conscientious in following the principles just outlined, we can stop worrying. We have an intercessor dwelling within, the Holy Spirit, who passes our requests through the grid of God's will, and the Father receives our requests through the mind of the Spirit (see Romans 8:27). Finally, we have an intercessor dwelling with the Father, the Lord Jesus Christ, who constantly pleads our case (see Romans 8:34; Hebrews 7:25; 1 John 2:1).

Reading the Bible mechanically, just sitting down and "putting in time," is not listening to God as He applies the truth of His Word to our lives. If we do not discern the will of God as we read His Word, we will not know what to pray for as we ought. The same Holy Spirit who dwells within us and intercedes for us when we pray is the One who will enable us to understand the truth of Scripture and who will apply it to our lives. As Jesus told His disciples:

"But the Helper, the Holy Spirit, whom the Father will send in My name, He will teach you all things, and bring to your remembrance all things that I said to you." (John 14:26)

When we turn the Word of God over and over in our minds and hearts, when we think about what it says, when we ponder the things the Holy Spirit is trying to teach us, when we reflect on its application to our lives, that is called *meditation*.

The Apostle Paul, in the same passage in which he urges us to bring everything to the Lord in prayer (see Philippians 4:6), also calls upon us to focus our thinking on the eternal truths found in God's Word:

"Finally, brethren, whatever things are true, whatever things are noble, whatever things are just, whatever things are pure, whatever things are lovely, whatever things are of good report, if there is any virtue and if there is anything praiseworthy—meditate on these things."
(Philippians 4:8)

Whatever we make the focus of our thinking soon becomes the basis of our behavior, as the psalmist suggests:

"I will meditate on Your precepts, and contemplate Your ways."
(Psalm 119:15)

The one who ponders the truth of God's Word and acts upon it is the one the Lord promises to bless (see Joshua 1:8; Psalm 1:1–3).

Another way to give the Holy Spirit an opportunity to teach us and lead us is to *memorize* passages of Scripture that we have already read and meditated upon (see Psalm 119:11). Later, when God wants to deal with us or give us a word to share with others, the Holy Spirit will bring to our remembrance what we have hidden in our hearts. That is why a memory verse is suggested for each of the weekly Bible readings in this *devotional prayer journal.*

WHY WE PRAY THE SCRIPTURES AND CLAIM THEM FOR OURSELVES

The primary reason why it is especially powerful to take the truth the Holy Spirit has taught us as we read, meditate upon, and memorize Scripture and then pray it back to the Lord during our devotions is that God promises to answer prayers based on His *revealed will!*:

"Now this is the confidence that we have in Him, that if we ask anything according to His will, He hears us. And if we know that He hears us, whatever we ask, we know that we have the petitions that we have asked of Him." (1 John 5:14–15)

God gives us an advance guarantee of positive answers to any prayers based on His known will as revealed in His Word, the Bible. That is one reason the Lord Jesus taught His disciples to pray that the heavenly Father's will be done on earth as it is in heaven (see Matthew 6:10).

One historical example that bears repeating is based on the commandment with promise that God the Father gives to God the Son in the Psalms:

"Ask of Me, and I will give You the nations for Your inheritance, and the ends of the earth for Your possession." (Psalm 2:8)

Taking this to be God's will in his life as well, the great Reformer, John Knox, prayed:

"Give me Scotland, or I die!"

Knox's passionate prayer was marvelously answered and the Presbyterian Church was born.

In addition to specific commandments, the entire Bible is full of *promises* that we may claim for ourselves. Both the Old and New Testaments make it clear that we can trust God to keep His promises because He is absolutely trustworthy and cannot lie (see Numbers 23:19; Titus 1:2). God promises to:

1. Give us eternal life if we trust Christ as Savior (John 1:12; 3:16)

2. Forgive our sins if we confess and forsake them (1 John 1:9)

3. Heal those for whom we pray in faith, in accordance with His will (James 5:14–15)

4. Meet all of our needs out of His riches in glory (Philippians 4:19)

5. Raise us up at the last day (John 6:39, 40, 44, 54)

What great and precious promises we have to claim (see 2 Peter 1:4)!

How To Make Personal Application and Record Personal Insights

One approach to making personal application of the Scripture is to ask ourselves a series of questions as we read and meditate on the Word of God. At the same time, we should pray that the Holy Spirit would open our minds to understand what we are reading, would teach us truths on which we can meditate, would convict us of changes we need to make in our lives, and would incline our wills to obey the will of God. We should ask such questions as:

1. What does God want me to *know* in this passage; what *truths* is He teaching me?

2. What does God want me to *be* or *become* in light of these truths?

3. What does God want me *think* or *feel* as a result of this passage?

4. What does God want me to *do*; how does He want me to *act* as a consequence of commandments in this passage?

5. What promises does God want me to *claim*; how does He want me to *pray* based on this passage?

Sometimes, the Holy Spirit will cause the lesson He wants to teach us virtually to leap off the page and enter our hearts and minds like a bolt of lightning! At other times, because of the circumstances of our lives, we will smile or break out laughing because the passage we are reading so perfectly fits our situation.

The lines printed on each page of this *devotional prayer journal* are provided so we may record personal insights, as we meditate, and the applications based on those insights. They may also be used to write specific prayer requests, and later the results of those requests. Suppose we have just read (and perhaps memorized) Philippians 4:19:

"And my God shall supply all your need according to His riches in glory by Christ Jesus."

Using the questions outlined above, I should meditate on this passage and ask the Holy Spirit to apply it to my life:

MEDITATION	APPLICATION
When God says "all" my need, He means all! If His riches are "by Christ Jesus," I know Jesus has all power in heaven and earth!	*Instead of worrying about my tax bill, I should go to the Lord and ask His help in meeting this need.*

I might then record a specific prayer request as a follow-up to the application:

PRAYER REQUEST	PRAYER RESULT
Lord, the tax bill needs to be paid, but I don't know where it's going to come from.	*Praise you, Lord! I didn't expect this insurance check for another month. What timing!*

By reviewing our prayer requests from time to time, we have an instant dated prayer list. We are also able to be reminded of God's past faithfulness and to be encouraged about the future, no matter what challenges we face.

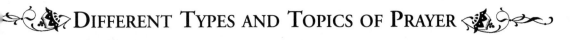

Unless we consciously include the different types of prayer (e.g., confession, thanksgiving, praise, supplication, intercession), as well as the different topics of prayer (e.g. for government leaders, family members, friends, healing, guidance, revival), in our devotional prayer times, we may omit certain vital aspects of our prayer life or find our prayers reduced to personal petitions at times of extremity. To aid the user of this journal to remember these various types and topics of prayer, and to provide models that we can use to get started each time, the following pages will be devoted to such models. Even the apostle Paul had to remind Timothy to maintain a balance in the prayer life of the church:

"Therefore I exhort first of all that supplications, prayers, intercessions, and giving of thanks be made for all men, for kings and all who are in authority, that we may lead a quiet and peaceable life in all godliness and reverence." (1 Timothy 2:1–2)

In other places, Paul would add poignantly: "And for me, . . ." (see Ephesians 6:19)

CONFESSION

There is a beautiful scene following the Lord's Supper that illustrates better than any explanation could the basic reason why we as Christians need to confess our sins daily. Jesus got up, laid aside His outer garments, and tied a towel around His waist. He then knelt down and proceeded to wash the disciples' feet, drying them with the towel. When He came to Peter, Peter protested and then asked Jesus to wash his hands and head as well (acknowledging his sinfulness by this request). Jesus' response to Peter sets forth the condition of a believer who has sinned as well as the remedy for this condition:

"Jesus said to him, 'He who is bathed needs only to wash his feet, but is completely clean; and you are clean, but not all of you.'" (John 13:10)

A believer has already been cleansed once completely when he or she first comes to Christ in repentance and receives Christ as Savior (1 John 1:9). Thereafter, when we sin, it is like an ancient traveler whose feet are dirty from walking on dusty roads in open sandals. When the traveler comes in off the road, he just needs to have his feet washed to be completely clean again. When we confess the particular sins we have committed since the last time we confessed, the Lord declares us forgiven and completely cleansed from all unrighteousness.

The effects of unconfessed and unforsaken sin for the believer are far more serious than unwashed feet! Since God made us to have fellowship with Himself, any sin in the life of a child of God has the effect of breaking fellowship between that person and his or her heavenly Father. Essentially, this was the experience Jesus had on the cross as He bore our sins and was the reason He cried out:

"My God, My God, why have You forsaken Me?" (Matthew 27:46)

His relationship with the Father was unbroken; He was still the son of God. But the communication lines were down since God is "of purer eyes than to behold evil" (Habakkuk 1:13). Our relationship with God remains secure, even when we sin. But we are no longer on speaking terms with Him and are not at that point usable in His service. How important it is to keep short accounts with God!

The Holy Spirit will show us those things in our lives that are displeasing to God, if we listen to Him as He applies God's Word to our hearts:

"And when He has come, He will convict the world of sin, and of righteousness, and of judgment." (John 16:8)

The following passages deal with confession and are followed by sample prayers that may help the reader get started in this area of prayer:

Scripture: "You ask and do not receive, because you ask amiss, that you may spend it on your pleasures." (James 4:3)

Prayer: Please forgive me for my self-centered prayers . . .

Scripture: "We have sinned and committed iniquity, we have done wickedly and rebelled, even by departing from Your precepts and Your judgments."(Daniel 9:5)

Prayer: Father, have mercy on America! . . .

Scripture: "For we do not have a High Priest who cannot sympathize with our weaknesses, but was in all points tempted as we are, yet without sin."(Hebrews 4:15)

Prayer: Lord Jesus, it is comforting to know You faced the same kind of temptation . . .

Scripture: "All we like sheep have gone astray; we have turned, everyone, to his own way; and the LORD has laid on Him the iniquity of us all." (Isaiah 53:6)

Prayer: When I consider what I've done, I feel so stupid sometimes . . .

Scripture: "No temptation has overtaken you except such as is common to man. . . ."(1 Corinthians 10:13)

Prayer: I should have been warned by the failure of others . . .

Scripture: "Therefore, to him who knows to do good and does not do it, to him it is sin."(James 4:17)

Prayer: It was within my power to help them, but I didn't . . .

Confession

Date	Name	Prayer Request	Prayer Result

Confession

Date	Name	Prayer Request	Prayer Result

Confession

Date	Name	Prayer Request	Prayer Result

Confession

Date	Name	Prayer Request	Prayer Result

Confession

Date	Name	Prayer Request	Prayer Result

Confession

Date	Name	Prayer Request	Prayer Result

Everything worthwhile in life, including life itself, is a gift of God:

> "Every good gift and every perfect gift is from above, and comes down from the Father of lights, with whom there is no variation or shadow of turning." (James 1:17)

When someone receives a gift, the most natural thing, indeed the expected thing, is to express gratitude to the giver. Perhaps that is why the Lord expressed surprise when only one out of ten lepers whom He cleansed bothered to return to give thanks, and that one was a Samaritan:

> "So Jesus answered and said, 'Were there not ten cleansed? But where are the nine? Were there not any found who returned to give glory to God except this foreigner?'" (Luke 17:17–18)

One sign of fallenness, of human beings in rebellion against God, is ingratitude. This was true at the beginning when human beings rejected the knowledge they had of the true God for that which is false:

> "Because, although they knew God, they did not glorify Him as God, nor were thankful. . . ." (Romans 1:21)

This will be true at the end when self-centered human beings regard themselves as self-sufficient:

> "For men will be lovers of themselves, lovers of money, boasters, proud, blasphemers, disobedient to parents, unthankful, unholy. . . ."(2 Timothy 3:2)

The opposite is true of a child of God. The believer knows where his or her blessings come from! In fact, when any really good thing happens to a Christian, the spontaneous response of his or her heart is to exult:

> "Thank you, Lord!"

The greatest tragedy for an unbeliever is to experience something special and have no one to thank.

Perhaps the most distinctive thing about a believer's gratitude is that it is possible to exult under really awful circumstances. Paul and Silas sang in prison (Acts 16:25), and Job blessed God after everything was taken away (Job 1:21). Paul summed it up well when he said:

"In everything give thanks; for this is the will of God in Christ Jesus for you." (1 Thessalonians 5:18)

Scripture: "The LORD will give strength to His people; the LORD will bless His people with peace." (Psalm 29:11)

Prayer: Thank You for giving me peace in the middle of the storm . . .

Scripture: "Bless the LORD, O my soul, and forget not all His benefits." (Psalm 103:2)

Prayer: Where do I begin to thank You for all You have done for me? . . .

Scripture: "But He was wounded for our transgressions, He was bruised for our iniquities; the chastisement for our peace was upon Him, and by His stripes we are healed." (Isaiah 53:5)

Prayer: Thank You for healing my soul . . .

Scripture: "It is good for me that I have been afflicted, That I may learn your statutes." (Psalm 119:71)

Prayer: Thank You for the lessons of Your discipline . . .

Scripture: "Giving thanks always for all things to God the Father in the name of our Lord Jesus Christ." (Ephesians 5:20)

Prayer: I can thank You even for this because I come to You in Jesus' name . . .

Thanksgiving

Date	Name	Prayer Request	Prayer Result

Thanksgiving

Date	Name	Prayer Request	Prayer Result

Thanksgiving

Date	Name	Prayer Request	Prayer Result

Thanksgiving

Date	Name	Prayer Request	Prayer Result

Thanksgiving

Date	Name	Prayer Request	Prayer Result

Thanksgiving

Date	Name	Prayer Request	Prayer Result

Praise is pure worship. Whereas thanksgiving is the believer's response to God for what He has done, praise is the believer's response to God for who He is. The two are closely related in many of the psalms:

"Enter into His gates with thanksgiving, and into His courts with praise. Be thankful to Him, and bless His name."(Psalm 100:4)

The angels of heaven likewise pour out their praise before God:

"All the angels stood around the throne and the elders and the four living creatures, and fell on their faces before the throne and worshiped God, saying: 'Amen! Blessing and glory and wisdom, thanksgiving and honor and power and might, be to our God forever and ever. Amen.'" (Revelation 7:11–12)

The prayer the Lord taught His disciples begins and ends with praise:

"Our Father in heaven, Hallowed be Your name. . . . For Yours is the kingdom and the power and the glory forever. Amen." (Matthew 6:9, 13)

The Westminister Shorter Catechism states it succinctly:

"The chief end of man is to glorify God and to enjoy Him forever."

Praise is the creature's response to the Creator. God alone is worthy of adoration. To worship anything or anyone else is idolatry. Again, such idolatry is another mark of fallen, rebellious creatures:

"Who exchanged the truth of God for the lie, and worshiped and served the creature rather than the Creator, who is blessed forever. Amen." (Romans 1:25)

It is significant that Satan's fall resulted from trying to displace the Creator as the object of worship. It is also significant that the devil tried to tempt Jesus to worship him, to which Jesus responded:

"Away with you, Satan! For it is written, 'You shall worship the LORD your God, and Him only you shall serve.'" (Matthew 4:10)

The irony is that we never rise so high as when we are on our face before the Lord. Worship lifts and ennobles us because it demonstrates that we are made in the image of God—made for worship and a personal relationship with our Creator. By contrast, nothing debases us so much as when we fail to honor the one true God.

Scripture: "For in him we live, and move and have our being, . . ." (Acts 17:28)

Prayer: I worship You as my creator and sustainer . . .

Scripture: "And you will seek Me and fine Me, when you search for Me with all your heart." (Jeremiah 29:13)

Prayer: O Lord, I adore You more than life itself . . .

Scripture: "My soul waits for the Lord more than those who watch for the morning. . . ." (Psalm 130:6)

Prayer: O Lord, I could not wait to have my devotions this morning! . . .

Scripture: "But you, when you pray, go into your room, and when you have shut your door, pray to your Father who is in the secret place. . . ." (Matthew 6:6)

Prayer: Lord, it is good to be alone with You . . .

Scripture: "He has put a new song in my mouth—Praise to our God. . . ." (Psalm 40:3)

Prayer: You alone make me break out into songs of praise . . .

Praise

Date	Name	Prayer Request	Prayer Result

Praise

Date	Name	Prayer Request	Prayer Result

Date	Name	Prayer Request	Prayer Result

Praise

Date	Name	Prayer Request	Prayer Result

Praise

Date	Name	Prayer Request	Prayer Result

Praise

Date	Name	Prayer Request	Prayer Result

Earlier, a definition of prayer was offered that begins:

"Prayer is asking God persistently . . ."

This definition relates more closely to supplication than to any other type of prayer. As Paul urges:

"Be anxious for nothing, but in everything by prayer and supplication, with thanksgiving, let your requests be made known to God." (Philippians 4:6)

Supplication is asking with a sense of urgency; it amounts to begging or beseeching. When we come to God with our petitions, it should never be casually or indifferently. Our whole heart and soul should be poured out before the Lord in earnest prayer.

In a sense, everything we ask God for could be considered supplication, and that is the use of the term in the acrostic A C T S. (Adoration, Confession, Thanksgiving, Supplication). Specifically, it includes all personal petitions, all requests to meet personal needs. It is with this large category of prayer in mind that the Lord teaches His disciples to pray:

"Give us this day our daily bread." (Matthew 6:11)

God wants to be involved in the everyday details of our lives. He wants us to come to Him with everything. Why? Because He loves us and delights to demonstrate His love in supplying our every need (see Philippians 4:19; 1 Peter 5:7).

Why do we not come to the Lord with all of our burdens and needs? There are two primary reasons: (1) we do not really want God's will in every situation (we have a better idea!); and (2) we do not really believe God loves us and has our best interests at heart. In the Sermon on the Mount, the Lord Jesus Christ deals with both reasons (or rather, rationalizations). On the first account, Jesus places a petition for the will of God to be done before the petition for God to meet our daily needs:

"Your kingdom come. Your will be done on earth as it is in heaven."
(Matthew 6:10)

In the second case, Jesus shames His disciples by pointing to God's care for birds and plants and then asking why they do not believe God would care for them (Matthew 6:26,30). He concludes by saying (really, commanding) that pursuing God's will ensures God's provision:

"But seek first the kingdom of God and His righteousness, and all these things shall be added to you." (Matthew 6:33)

Scripture: "Ask, and it will be given to you; seek, and you will find; knock, and it will be opened to you." (Matthew 7:7)

Prayer: Lord, I'm asking . . .

Scripture: "I have been young, and now am old; yet I have not seen the righteous forsaken, nor his descendants begging bread." (Psalm 37:25)

Prayer: O Father, I have lost my job and need to feed my family . . .

Scripture: "And when they had prayed, the place where they were assembled together was shaken; and they were all filled with the Holy Spirit. . . ."
(Acts 4:31)

Prayer: Father, send a Holy Ghost revival to our church! . . .

Scripture: "And when He had sent the multitudes away, He went up on the mountain by Himself to pray. . . ." (Matthew 14:23)

Prayer: The world crowds in, and I need a touch from You . . .

Scripture: "But you, beloved, building yourselves up on your most holy faith, praying in the Holy Spirit." (Jude 20)

Prayer: Holy Spirit, make up what is lacking in my prayer . . .

Supplication

Date	Name	Prayer Request	Prayer Result

Supplication

Date	Name	Prayer Request	Prayer Result

Supplication

Date	Name	Prayer Request	Prayer Result

Supplication

Date	Name	Prayer Request	Prayer Result

Supplication

Date	Name	Prayer Request	Prayer Result

Supplication

Date	Name	Prayer Request	Prayer Result

A special form of prayer or supplication is prayer on behalf of others. Such prayer is called intercession. Aside from pure worship (praise or adoration) of God Himself, there is no nobler type of prayer than to intercede before God on behalf of the needs of others. In the Old Testament, this was a special responsibility of prophets. Even when Israel sinned against God by asking for a king, Samuel did not abandon his role as an intercessor for the nation:

"Moreover, as for me, far be it from me that I should sin against the LORD in ceasing to pray for you. . . ." (1 Samuel 12:23)

Later on, when Israel faced extinction as a nation, God saw there were no faithful prophets interceding for His people:

"He saw that there was no man, and wondered that there was no intercessor. . . ." (Isaiah 59:16)

In the New Testament, the responsibility for intercessory prayer is extended to all believers:

"Therefore I exhort first of all that supplications, prayers, intercessions, and giving of thanks be made for all men." (1 Timothy 2:1)

Over and over again in his letters, Paul shares with the churches that he is praying for them:

"[I] do not cease to give thanks for you, making mention of you in my prayers." (Ephesians 1:16)

Having said this, we need to examine our commitment in saying to others, "I'm praying for you." We must faithfully intercede for them, and not just express polite words of concern. They are counting on us!

For the Christian, the most significant intercessory prayer that goes on is the ministry performed on our behalf by the Holy Spirit and the Lord

Jesus Christ. In the case of the Holy Spirit, we are told:

"Likewise the Spirit also helps in our weaknesses. For we do not know what we should pray for as we ought, but the Spirit Himself makes intercession for us with groanings which cannot be uttered."(Romans 8:26)

In addition, the Lord Jesus is "even at the right hand of God, who also makes intercession for us" (Romans 8:34). We count on Their intercession; others count on us.

Scripture: "Therefore I exhort first of all that supplications, prayers, intercessions, and giving of thanks be made for all men." (1 Timothy 2:1)

> *Prayer:* Lord, You know who is weighing heavily on my heart right now . . .

Scripture: "Peter was therefore kept in prison, but constant prayer was offered to God for him by the church." (Acts 12:5)

> *Prayer:* Lord, please protect . . .

Scripture: "For I was hungry and you gave Me no food; I was thirsty and you gave Me no drink." (Matthew 25:42)

> *Prayer:* Father, give me compassion for the starving of this world . . .

Scripture: "Brethren, pray for us." (1 Thessalonians 5:25)

> *Prayer:* Father, I pray you will take away the suffering of . . .

Scripture: "Praying always . . . in the Spirit, . . . for all the saints—and for me. . . ." (Ephesians 6:18,19)

> *Prayer:* Father, give our pastor boldness to proclaim the gospel on Sunday . . .

Intercession

Date	Name	Prayer Request	Prayer Result

Intercession

Date	Name	Prayer Request	Prayer Result

Intercession

Date	Name	Prayer Request	Prayer Result

Intercession

Date	Name	Prayer Request	Prayer Result

Intercession

Date	Name	Prayer Request	Prayer Result

Intercession

Date	Name	Prayer Request	Prayer Result

Not only are there specific types of prayer we should incorporate into our devotions, but there are specific topics of prayer — matters for which and persons for whom — we should be praying on a regular basis. They include the fruit of the Spirit — love, joy, peace, etc. —, and specific issues and needs — temptation, comfort, healing, financial needs, the unsaved, etc. They also include specific individuals — spouse, parents, children, political leaders, church leaders, missionaries, colleagues, friends, enemies, etc. Since the subject of intercessory prayer has just been dealt with and illustrated, this section will consider the three fruits of the spirit listed above as well as the five issues and needs mentioned. Other matters will be brought to our minds by the Holy Spirit as we have our devotions.

The main reason we should pray for these various topics is that we are commanded to do so. Even in the case of the fruit of the Spirit — love, joy, peace, etc. — God commands us to exhibit these character traits. We all face temptation on a daily basis and this was one topic Jesus included in the model prayer He taught His disciples:

"And do not lead us into temptation, but deliver us from the evil." (Matthew 6:13)

Bereavement is another universal human experience, and we are to "weep with those who weep" (Romans 12:15). As we comfort others, we know we have the Comforter Himself dwelling within us (John 14:16–17). Illness is still another occasion for us to minister to one another. Again, we are commanded to pray for healing and health (James 5:16). A catastrophic illness, the loss of a job, the general economy — all of these things can throw our budgets into a tail spin. God wants us to trust Him and come to Him to meet our financial needs as well, and He will (Philippians 4:19). Finally, we are commanded in the Great Commission to go into all the world and reach the lost for Christ (Matthew 28:19–20). In all of these areas, God wants us to pray specifically. If we do not, we will not receive specific answers:

"You do not have because you do not ask." (James 4:2)

∽ LOVE ∼

Scripture: "A new commandment I give to you, that you love one another; as I have loved you, that you also love one another." (John 13:34)

Prayer: Help me to show love to others by serving them, . . .

Scripture: "Love suffers long and is kind; love does not envy; love does not parade itself, is not puffed up." (1 Corinthians 13:4)

Prayer: I confess that my expressions of love have been far too selfish and self-seeking . . .

Scripture: "In this is love, not that we loved God, but that He loved us and sent His Son to be the propitiation for our sins." (1 John 4:10)

Prayer: Father, I praise You for sending Jesus to die for my sins . . .

Scripture: "You shall love your neighbor as yourself." (Matthew 19:19)

Prayer: Forgive me, Lord. I've lived next door to . . . all these years and have not witnessed to them as I should . . .

Scripture: "But I say to you who hear: Love your enemies, do good to those who hate you." (Luke 6:27)

Prayer: I have been so bitter against . . . Show me something concrete I can do to bless him/her . . .

Scripture: "For the love of Christ compels us, because we judge thus: that if One died for all, then all died." (2 Corinthians 5:14)

Prayer: If You loved me enough to die for me, how can I do less than live for You? . . .

SPECIFIC PRAYERS
Love

Date	Prayer Request	Date Answered

SPECIFIC PRAYERS
Love

Date	Prayer Request	Date Answered

❦ Joy ❦

Scripture: "These things I have spoken to you, that My joy may remain in you, and that your joy may be full." (John 15:11)

Prayer: I thank you for sharing Your joy with me through Your Word . .

Scripture: "Rejoice in the Lord always. Again I will say, rejoice!" (Philippians 4:4)

Prayer: No matter what the circumstances, You give me cause for joy . . .

Scripture: "My brethren, count it all joy when you fall into various trials." (James 1:2)

Prayer: Lord, help me to rejoice just in knowing that You are using these trials to strengthen my faith . . .

Scripture: "[Jesus] whom having not seen you love. Though now you do not see Him, yet believing, you rejoice with joy inexpressible and full of glory." (1 Peter 1:8)

Prayer: When I remember the day I first trusted in You, my heart is filled to overflowing with the joy I felt then . . .

Scripture: "Looking unto Jesus, the author and finisher of our faith, who for the joy that was set before Him endured the cross. . . ." (Hebrews 12:2)

Prayer: To think that the joy of my salvation was enough for You to be willing to go to the cross! . . .

Scripture: "You will show me the path of life; in Your presence is fullness of joy; at Your right hand are pleasure forevermore." (Psalm 16:11)

Prayer: This world has nothing to compare with the joy of being in Your presence. It's a taste of heaven right here and now . . .

SPECIFIC PRAYERS
Joy

Date	Prayer Request	Date Answered

SPECIFIC PRAYERS
Joy

Date	Prayer Request	Date Answered

Scripture: "Peace I leave with you, My peace I give to you; not as the world gives do I give to you. Let not your heart be troubled, neither let it be afraid." (John 14:27)

   Prayer: Please forgive me for being so anxious instead of claiming Your promise of peace . . .

Scripture: "For He Himself is our peace, who has made both one, and has broken down the middle wall of separation." (Ephesians 2:14)

   Prayer: Thank you, Lord, for making me Your friend when I was Your enemy . . .

Scripture: "If it is possible, as much as depends on you, live peaceably with all men." (Romans 12:18)

   Prayer: Father, may I be a peacemaker and not a troublemaker . . .

Scripture: "And the peace of God, which surpasses all understanding, will guard your hearts and minds through Christ Jesus." (Philippians 4:7)

   Prayer: Lord, I thank You for listening while I poured out my heart. I feel such a peace, and the fear is gone . . .

Scripture: "The things which you learned and received and heard and saw in me, these do, and the God of peace will be with you." (Philippians 4:9)

   Prayer: Now I understand. You bring peace to me when I am obedient to You . . .

SPECIFIC PRAYERS
Peace

Date	Prayer Request	Date Answered

SPECIFIC PRAYERS
Peace

Date	Prayer Request	Date Answered

Scripture: "No temptation has overtaken you except such as is common to man; but God is faithful, who will not allow you to be tempted beyond what you are able, but with the temptation will also make the way of escape, that you may be able to bear it." (1 Corinthians 10:13)

> *Prayer:* Lord, I confess I have persisted in my sin even when You have made a way of escape . . .

Scripture: "For we do not have a High Priest who cannot sympathize with our weaknesses, but was in all points tempted as we are, yet without sin." (Hebrews 4:15)

> *Prayer:* How thankful I am that You know what I am struggling with, and that because of You I do not have to be defeated . . .

Scripture: "Therefore we also, since we are surrounded by so great a cloud of witnesses, let us lay aside every weight, and the sin which so easily ensnares us. . . ." (Hebrews 12:1)

> *Prayer:* Lord, when I am tempted, remind me of how many people are looking to my example, . . .

Scripture: "Do not love the world or the things in the world. If anyone loves the world, the love of the Father is not in him." (1 John 2:15)

> *Prayer:* I have to admit it. This temptation's allure shows me that at times I love the world more than I love You . . .

Scripture: "But each one is tempted when he is drawn away by his own desires and enticed." (James 1:14)

> *Prayer:* I can't point my finger anywhere else. My own heart is corrupt . . .

SPECIFIC PRAYERS
Temptation

Date	Prayer Request	Date Answered

SPECIFIC PRAYERS
Temptation

Date	Prayer Request	Date Answered

Scripture: "In My Father's house are many mansions; if it were not so, I would have told you. I go to prepare a place for you." (John 14:2)

> *Prayer:* Lord Jesus, I am overwhelmed to think You are not only preparing a home for Your children in heaven but a specific place of service . . .

Scripture: "Jesus said to her, 'I am the resurrection and the life. He who believes in Me, though he may die, he shall live.'" (John 11:25)

> *Prayer:* Thank You, Lord, for the assurance that because You have risen from the dead, we too shall be resurrected at the last day . . .

Scripture: "And God will wipe away every tear from their eyes; there shall be no more death, nor sorrow, nor crying. There shall be no more pain, for the former things have passed away." (Revelation 21:4)

> *Prayer:* What a joy to know that our loved ones' suffering is over forever! . . .

Scripture: "Jesus wept." (John 11:35)

> *Prayer:* Lord, I know You can feel my pain . . .

Scripture: "But I do not want you to be ignorant, brethren, concerning those who have fallen asleep, lest you sorrow as others who have no hope." (1 Thessalonians 4:13)

> *Prayer:* Thank You, Lord, for the promise that we will see our loved ones again . . .

Scripture: "[Jesus Christ] who died for us, that whether we wake or sleep, we should live together with Him." (1 Thessalonians 5:10)

> *Prayer:* What a thought! To live forever with Jesus! . . .

SPECIFIC PRAYERS
Comfort

Date	Prayer Request	Date Answered

SPECIFIC PRAYERS
Comfort

Date	Prayer Request	Date Answered

Scripture: ". . . pray for one another, that you may be healed. The effective, fervent prayer of a righteous man avails much." (James 5:16)

> *Prayer:* In obedience to Your command, I ask for Your healing touch upon . . .

Scripture: "Bless the LORD, O my soul, and forget not all His benefits; . . . who heals all your diseases." (Psalm 103:2–3)

> *Prayer:* Thank You, Lord, for guiding the doctor's hands . . .

Scripture: ". . . I was sick and you visited Me. . . ." (Matthew 25:36)

> *Prayer:* Now I know the true significance of making those hospital visits . . .

Scripture: "And He said to me, 'My grace is sufficient for you, for My strength is made perfect in weakness.' Therefore most gladly I will rather boast in my infirmities, that the power of Christ may rest upon me." (2 Corinthians 12:9)

> *Prayer:* Whether You choose to heal me or not, I want everyone to see Your strength in my life . . .

Scripture: "Is anyone among you sick? Let him call for the elders of the church, and let them pray over him. . . ." (James 5:14)

> *Prayer:* I've been putting it off, but I'm going to call the pastor and ask for prayer . . .

Scripture: "I said, 'LORD, be merciful to me; Heal my soul, for I have sinned against You.'" (Psalm 41:4)

> *Prayer:* O Lord, heal my sin-sick soul . . .

SPECIFIC PRAYERS
Healing

Date	Prayer Request	Date Answered

SPECIFIC PRAYERS
Healing

Date	Prayer Request	Date Answered

Scripture: "The blessing of the LORD makes one rich, and He adds no sorrow with it." (Proverbs 10:22)

> *Prayer:* O Lord, You are the source of every material blessing; I need not feel guilty for what You place in my hands . . .

Scripture: "And you shall remember the LORD your God, for it is He who gives you power to get wealth. . . ." (Deuteronomy 8:18)

> *Prayer:* Father, please forgive me for taking the credit for what You have enabled me to earn . . .

Scripture: "Command those who are rich in this present age not to be haughty, nor to trust in uncertain riches but in the living God, who gives us richly all things to enjoy." (1 Timothy 6:17)

> *Prayer:* Lord, help me to remember that "In God We Trust" is not just a motto on our coins . . .

Scripture: "And my God shall supply all your need according to His riches in glory by Christ Jesus." (Philippians 4:19)

> *Prayer:* Father, You know my financial needs right now, and You have promised to meet them . . .

Scripture: "And God is able to make all grace abound toward you, that you, always having all sufficiency in all things, may have an abundance for every good work." (2 Corinthians 9:8)

> *Prayer:* How wonderful to know that You will always provide enough for me to be able to give to Your work as well as meet my need . . .

SPECIFIC PRAYERS
Financial Needs

Date	Prayer Request	Date Answered

SPECIFIC PRAYERS
Financial Needs

Date	Prayer Request	Date Answered

Scripture: "Go therefore and make disciples of all the nations, baptizing them in the name of the Father and of the Son and of the Holy Spirit." (Matthew 28:19)

Prayer: Here I am, Lord; send me. . .

Scripture: "For 'whoever calls on the name of the LORD shall be saved.'" (Romans 10:13)

Prayer: Help me to remember that people need to hear about Jesus. . .

Scripture: "But you shall receive power when the Holy Spirit has come upon you; and you shall be witnesses to Me. . . ." (Acts 1:8)

Prayer: Give me a holy boldness in witnessing. . .

Scripture: "For the Son of Man has come to seek and to save that which was lost." (Luke 19:10)

Prayer: If it was Jesus' purpose to reach the lost, then it is mine too. . .

Scripture: "And you He made alive, who were dead in trespasses and sins." (Ephesians 2:1)

Prayer: May I never forget I was once lost. . .

Scripture: "I say to you that likewise there will be more joy in heaven over one sinner who repents. . . ." (Luke 15:7)

Prayer: To think you and the angels throw a party in heaven every time someone accepts Christ!. . .

SPECIFIC PRAYERS
The Unsaved

Date	Prayer Request	Date Answered

SPECIFIC PRAYERS
The Unsaved

Date	Prayer Request	Date Answered

We approach the Bible as we do no other book. The Bible is God's inspired, inerrant Word. Everything it affirms is true and relevant to our lives. Our attitude as we prepare ourselves to study the Scripture should be one of expectancy and excitement:

"Your words were found, and I ate them, and Your word was to me the joy and rejoicing of my heart. . . ." (Jeremiah 15:16)

The more time we spend in the Word, the more we come to love it and the more it comes to fill our minds and hearts:

"Oh, how I love your law! It is my meditation all the day." (Psalm 119:97)

We should come to be known individually and collectively as people of the Book.

There are many helps to Bible study, and many good Bible teachers. But when it comes to a devotional study of the Word of God, we have one Helper and Teacher who excels them all—the Holy Spirit:

"But the Helper, the Holy Spirit, whom the Father will send in My name, He will teach you all things, and bring to your remembrance all things that I said to you." (John 14:26)

What the Holy Spirit inspired in the writers of Scripture was truth from beginning to end, and what He teaches us is truth and is about the One who is the Truth:

"However, when He, the Spirit of truth, has come, He will guide you into all truth. . . . He will glorify Me, for He will take of what is Mine and declare it to you." (John 16:13–14)

Christ is the grand subject of Scripture, and since Christ is "the same yesterday, today, and forever" (Hebrews 13:8), we should expect the message of the Bible to be consistent throughout. The truth is the truth, and the same for everyone. While applications may vary according to the circumstances of our lives and what God is trying to teach us individually, the truth will not.

While most devotionals just leap off from some text, the devotionals in this journal do not. They provide the reader with a mini-commentary on the whole New Testament as they highlight the high points from each week's readings. Complementary Old Testament readings are suggested that further illuminate the daily New Testament readings.

As we meditate upon the daily readings from the Old and New Testaments, we should remember that the Scripture has different functions and these functions are reflected in metaphors used by the Bible to describe itself:

Life	The words of Scripture produce eternal life in the first place (1 Peter 1:23); they purify and mature our Christian lives in the second place (Ephesians 5:26; 1 Peter 2:2).
Light	The words of the Bible give us understanding of the truth (Psalm 119:130); they also illuminate the path of life by teaching us how to live (Psalm 119:105).
Mirror	The Word of God shows us ourselves as we really are; but we are to act on what we see and not forget the images God shows us (James 1:23, 24).
Sword	The Word of God is called "the sword of the Spirit" (Ephesians 6:17) and is the one offensive piece of the Christian's armor; God also uses it on us to lay us bare before Him (Hebrews 4:12, 13).
Bread	Scripture feeds our souls, nourishes our spiritual lives, as bread feeds our bodies (Deuteronomy 8:3; Matthew 4:4); Christ calls Himself the bread of heaven which we must eat to live (John 6:51, 58, 63).

Fire   Like a fire, God's Word consumes whatever is false or evil (Jeremiah 5:14); the Holy Spirit causes the truth of Scripture to burn within our hearts (Luke 24:32).

Hammer   The power of the Word of God to humble and convict of sin may be compared to a hammer breaking rocks apart (Jeremiah 23:29); Scripture is profitable for reproof and correction (2 Timothy 3:16).

We can expect the Bible to have all of these functions and more in our lives. A devotional study of the Word of God is anything but dull!

DEVOTIONAL: The miracle of Jesus' birth, the wonder of His miracles, the power of His preaching — all of these together argue for His uniqueness as the Son of God. They also make His commands for us to let our light shine (Matthew 5:16) and to exceed the self-righteousness of the Pharisees (Matthew 5:20) the revealed will of God Himself for godly living. Jesus' moral teachings went deeper and further than the hypocritical legalists of His day. They combine the standard of God's perfection (Matthew 5:48) with the compassion of His loving heart (Matthew 5:44), a perfect balance for living.

New Testament	Old Testament
Monday: Matthew 1:1–25	Isaiah 7:10–14; Genesis 17:1–8; 18:17–18
Meditation:_____	Application: _____
_____	_____
_____	_____
_____	_____
Tuesday: Matthew 2:1–23	Psalm 57:1–11
Meditation:_____	Application: _____
_____	_____
_____	_____
_____	_____
Wednesday: Matthew 3:1–4:11	Psalm 34:1–14
Meditation:_____	Application: _____
_____	_____
_____	_____
_____	_____

Thursday: Matthew 4:12–5:12

Meditation:_____

_____

_____

_____

Genesis 12:1–4; Isaiah 6:1–8

Application: _____

_____

_____

_____

Friday: Matthew 5:13–37

Meditation:_____

_____

_____

_____

Psalm 89:11–15; 97:10–11;
18:28

Application: _____

_____

_____

_____

Weekend: Matthew 5:38–6:15

Meditation:_____

_____

_____

_____

Psalm 25:1–18

Application: _____

_____

_____

_____

MEMORY VERSE: Let your light so shine before men, that they may see your good works, and glorify your Father in heaven. Matthew 5:16

DEVOTIONAL: Jesus established the right priorities for His church: seeking (Matthew 6:33) and doing (Matthew 7:21) the will of God; seeing a lost world (Matthew 8:11) in need of forgiveness (Matthew 9:6); and answering God's call to enter the harvest as colaborers with Christ (Matthew 9:37–38). We will suffer persecution as Christians in this world (Matthew 10:22), but the Lord encourages us by telling us of the Holy Spirit's help (Matthew 10:20) and of the Father's power (Matthew 10:28). Let us ask Him to show us His plan for a dying world, and then get in on it!

New Testament	Old Testament
Monday. Matthew 6:16–7:6	Nehemiah 9:1–3; Joel 2:12–13; Zechariah 7:1–6
Meditation:_____	Application: _____
_____	_____
_____	_____
_____	_____
Tuesday. Matthew 7:7–8:4	Psalm 1:1–3; 37:23, 24; Ezekiel 33:30–33
Meditation:_____	Application: _____
_____	_____
_____	_____
_____	_____
Wednesday. Matthew 8:5–27	Psalm 104:1–9, 27–33
Meditation:_____	Application: _____
_____	_____
_____	_____
_____	_____

Thursday. Matthew 8:28–9:17

Psalm 32:1–7; 103:8–13

Meditation:_____

Application: _____

_____

_____

_____

_____

_____

_____

Friday. Matthew 9:18–10:10

Psalm 103:1–5; Ezekiel 34:11–16

Meditation:_____

Application: _____

_____

_____

_____

_____

_____

_____

Weekend. Matthew 10:11–40

Psalm 119:41–46; Jeremiah 20:7–9

Meditation:_____

Application: _____

_____

_____

_____

_____

_____

_____

MEMORY VERSE: But seek first the kingdom of God and His righteousness, and all these things shall be added to you. Matthew 6:33

DEVOTIONAL: Spiritual blindness is an awful thing. It led the people of Jesus' day to ascribe the ministry of John the Baptist (Matthew 11:18) and the miracles of Jesus (Matthew 12:24) to the devil. It also accounts for why Jesus taught in parables (Matthew 13:13). The Holy Spirit opens our eyes to understand God's Word (Matthew 13:11, 23) and our hearts to receive Christ (Matthew 12:18–21). God's judgment on those who have rejected Christ is also an awful thing, as the parables of the wheat and the tares (Matthew 13:41–42) and of the fishing net (Matthew 13:49–50) illustrate.

New Testament	Old Testament
Monday. Matthew 10:41–11:24	Proverbs 1:22–31; Malachi 3:1
Meditation:_____	Application: _____
_____	_____
_____	_____
_____	_____
Tuesday. Matthew 11:25–12:21	Psalm 51:17; Deuteronomy 10:12–13, 16, 20–21; Micah 6:6–8
Meditation:_____	Application: _____
_____	_____
_____	_____
_____	_____
Wednesday. Matthew 12:22–45	Proverbs 10:20–21; 15:3–4, 26; Psalm 15
Meditation:_____	Application: _____
_____	_____
_____	_____
_____	_____

Thursday. Matthew 12:46–13:17

Psalm 119:97–106; Jeremiah 25:4–5, 7; Ezekiel 12:1–2

Meditation:_____

Application: _____

_____

_____

_____

_____

_____

_____

Friday. Matthew 13:18–43

Deuteronomy 11:18–19; Proverbs 2:1–5; Psalm 119:10–16

Meditation:_____

Application: _____

_____

_____

_____

_____

_____

_____

Weekend. Matthew 13:44–14:12

Isaiah 9:6–7; Psalm 96:10–13; 145:10–13

Meditation:_____

Application: _____

_____

_____

_____

_____

_____

_____

_____

_____

MEMORY VERSE: Come to Me, all you who labor and are heavy laden, and I will give you rest. Matthew 11:28

DEVOTIONAL: Even though Jesus fed two multitudes to satisfy the hunger of their stomachs (Matthew 14:19; 15:36), He was far more interested in the condition of their hearts (Matthew 15:18). He condemned the external religiosity of the Jewish leaders of His day (Matthew 16:12), and He commended Peter's confession of faith (Matthew 16:16–18). To be His disciples, we must humble ourselves (Matthew 16:24) and have the faith of a child (Matthew 18:3). In our relationships with one another, we must be redemptive (Matthew 18:15) and forgiving (Matthew 18:35). Has Christ become Lord of our hearts and our relationships?

New Testament	Old Testament
Monday. Matthew 14:13–36	Psalm 111:1–5; 116:1–9; Isaiah 26:3–4; Haggai 2:4–5
Meditation:_____	Application: _____
Tuesday. Matthew 15:1–31	Proverbs 26:24–26; 30:11–13; Isaiah 29:13–14
Meditation:_____	Application: _____
Wednesday. Matthew 15:32–16:20	Numbers 11:21–23, 31–32; Isaiah 55:1–2
Meditation:_____	Application: _____

Thursday. Matthew 16:21–17:13

Psalm 62:11–12; Isaiah 53:6–10;
Daniel 12:1–3

Meditation:————————

Application: ————————

————————————
————————————
————————————

————————————
————————————
————————————

Friday. Matthew 17:14–18:9

Psalm 138:1–6; Proverbs 29:23;
2 Chronicles 33:12–13

Meditation:————————

Application: ————————

————————————
————————————
————————————

————————————
————————————
————————————

Weekend. Matthew 18:10–35

Ezekiel 18:21–23; Psalm 51:1–11

Meditation:————————

Application: ————————

————————————
————————————
————————————
————————————

————————————
————————————
————————————
————————————

MEMORY VERSE: Then Jesus said to His disciples, "If anyone desires to come after Me, let him deny himself, and take up his cross, and follow Me." Matthew 16:24

DEVOTIONAL: How people respond to Jesus determines their eternal destiny. The rich young man turned away sorrowful because of his possessions (Matthew 19:22). The disciples forsook all and were blessed (Matthew 19:28). The mother of James and John sought prominence for her sons and was corrected (Matthew 20:23). The crowd who accepted Him cried Hosanna (Matthew 21:9), and the Jewish leaders who rejected Him were angry (Matthew 21:15). Jesus becomes either the corner stone or the crushing stone (Matthew 21:44). The key to people's response is whether they accept or reject the truth of Scripture (Matthew 22:29). What is our response?

New Testament	Old Testament
Monday. Matthew 19:1–26	Malachi 2:13–16; Genesis 2:19–24
Meditation:_____	Application: _____
_____	_____
_____	_____
_____	_____
Tuesday. Matthew 19:27–20:19	1 Samuel 2:2–10
Meditation:_____	Application: _____
_____	_____
_____	_____
_____	_____
Wednesday. Matthew 20:20–21:11	Psalm 95:1–3; 118:24–27; Isaiah 62:8–10
Meditation:_____	Application: _____
_____	_____
_____	_____
_____	_____

Thursday. Matthew 21:12–32

Psalm 26:8; Jeremiah 7:10–14; Isaiah 56:7

Meditation:_____

Application: _____

_____

_____

_____

_____

_____

_____

Friday. Matthew 21:33–22:14

Isaiah 56:3–5; Psalm 103:15–22

Meditation:_____

Application: _____

_____

_____

_____

_____

_____

_____

Weekend. Matthew 22:15–40

Deuteronomy 6:4–9; 7:9–11; Joshua 22:1–2, 5; Proverbs 8:17

Meditation:_____

Application: _____

_____

_____

_____

_____

_____

_____

_____

_____

MEMORY VERSE: So the last will be first, and the first last. For many are called, but few chosen. Matthew 20:16

DEVOTIONAL: Jesus' teaching about His second coming was meant to do two things: to encourage His own to finish His work of proclaiming the gospel to all peoples (Matthew 24:14), and to exhort us to be ready whenever He returns (Matthew 24:44). For when the judgment comes, He will examine our lives to see if we have been faithful to use the gifts He has given us in His service (Matthew 25:21,23). We will be held accountable for the light we have. Judas's betrayal was with knowledge (Matthew 26:2). How much more accountable will we be with all the light we have? Are we ready for His return?

New Testament	Old Testament
Monday. Matthew 22:41–23:22	Ezekiel 13:8–16
Meditation:_____	Application: _____
_____	_____
_____	_____
_____	_____
Tuesday. Matthew 23:23–24:8	Jeremiah 2:30, 34–35; Psalm 94:20–23
Meditation:_____	Application: _____
_____	_____
_____	_____
_____	_____
Wednesday. Matthew 24:9–35	Daniel 7:13–14; Isaiah 13:9–10; 34:1–4
Meditation:_____	Application: _____
_____	_____
_____	_____
_____	_____

Thursday. Matthew 24:36–25:13

Malachi 3:1–5, 14–18;
Zephaniah 2:1–3

Meditation:_____

Application: _____

_____

_____

_____

_____

_____

_____

Friday. Matthew 25:14–40

Psalm 41:1–3; 112:5–9;
Proverbs 14:31; 19:17

Meditation:_____

Application: _____

_____

_____

_____

_____

_____

_____

Weekend. Matthew 25:41–26:19

Judges 13:15–23; Genesis
8:18–21

Meditation:_____

Application: _____

_____

_____

_____

_____

_____

_____

MEMORY VERSE: And this gospel of the kingdom will be preached in all the world as a witness to all the nations, and then the end will come. Matthew 24:14

DEVOTIONAL: The events that transpired at the end of Jesus' earthly ministry, from the betrayal (Matthew 26:1–3), to the mock trial (Matthew 26:59–68), to Pilate's final decision to hand Jesus over for crucifixion (Matthew 27:24–26), to the details of His death on the cross (Matthew 27:35), to His burial (Matthew 28:6), all happened according to God's plan and Scriptural prophecy. Jesus did not have His life taken away; He gave it willingly for us (Matthew 26:39). After His resurrection, He gave us the Great Commission (Matthew 28:19–20), along with His promise never to leave us or forsake us (Matthew 28:20).

<table>
<tr><th>New Testament</th><th>Old Testament</th></tr>
</table>

Monday. Matthew 26:20–46

Psalm 73:1–5; Zechariah 13:7–9; Ezekiel 34:11–13, 16

Meditation:—————————

Application: —————————

_____

_____

_____

_____

_____

_____

Tuesday. Matthew 26:47–68

Psalm 55:12–14, 20–21; Judges 7:2–3; Job 19:13–19

Meditation:—————————

Application: —————————

_____

_____

_____

_____

_____

_____

Wednesday. Matthew 26:69–27:20

Daniel 2:26–28; 4:24–27

Meditation:—————————

Application: —————————

_____

_____

_____

_____

_____

_____

Thursday. Matthew 27:21–44

Psalm 22:6–8; 42:1–4; 44:13–16;
Isaiah 53:1–3, 5

Meditation:_____

Application: _____

_____

_____

_____

_____

_____

_____

Friday. Matthew 27:45–28:10

Psalm 68:16–20; 16:8–10

Meditation:_____

Application: _____

_____

_____

_____

_____

_____

_____

Weekend. Matthew 28:11–Mark 1:20

1 Chronicles 16:23–25;
Isaiah 61:1–3

Meditation:_____

Application: _____

_____

_____

_____

_____

_____

_____

MEMORY VERSES: Go therefore and make disciples of all the nations, baptizing them in the name of the Father and of the Son and of the Holy Spirit, teaching them to observe all things that I have commanded you; and lo, I am with you always, even to the end of the age. Amen. Matthew 28:19–20

DEVOTIONAL: Mark's Gospel launches us almost immediately into Jesus' Galilean ministry. He taught (Mark 1:22) and healed (Mark 1:27) with the authority of God Himself. He was criticized for declaring sins forgiven (Mark 2:7), for eating with sinners (Mark 2:16), and for healing on the Sabbath (Mark 3:2). He taught in parables (Mark 4:11), but explained everything to His disciples (Mark 4:34). He calmed the elements (Mark 4:41) and cast out demons (Mark 5:8). In every case, He demonstrated compassion, as in the healing of the woman with the issue of blood (Mark 5:26–34). Oh, how He loves you and me!

New Testament	Old Testament
Monday. Mark 1:21–45	Psalm 31:14–16; 145:8–9; Isaiah 30:18; Hosea 6:1–3
Meditation:_____	Application: _____
Tuesday. Mark 2:1–22	Isaiah 43:22–25; 53:10–12
Meditation:_____	Application: _____
Wednesday. Mark 2:23–3:27	1 Samuel 21:1–5; Isaiah 56:2
Meditation:_____	Application: _____

Thursday. Mark 3:28–4:20

Exodus 19:3–5; Deuteronomy 28:1–10

Meditation:_____

Application: _____

_____

_____

_____

_____

_____

_____

Friday. Mark 4:21–5:10

Psalm 29:3–5, 7, 10; 77:11–19

Meditation:_____

Application: _____

_____

_____

_____

_____

_____

_____

Weekend. Mark 5:11–36

1 Samuel 17:42–47, 50;
1 Kings 18:25–29

Meditation:_____

Application: _____

_____

_____

_____

_____

_____

_____

MEMORY VERSE: When Jesus heard it, He said to them, "Those who are well have no need of a physician, but those who are sick. I did not come to call the righteous, but sinners, to repentance." Mark 2:17

DEVOTIONAL: People were constantly, and mistakenly, judging Jesus by externals. The people of Nazareth did so because of familiarity (Mark 6:4). The 5,000 did so because they were fed (Mark 6:41). The scribes and Pharisees did so on the basis of their traditions (Mark 7:8–9). Jesus said our problems are internal, of the heart. The disciples' hearts were hardened on occasion (Mark 6:52). The leaders' hearts were far from God (Mark 7:6). It is what comes out of the heart that defiles us (Mark 7:20–23), including our valuing people's opinions more than God's (Mark 8:36–38). Where are our hearts fixed?

New Testament	Old Testament
Monday. Mark 5:37–6:20	Deuteronomy 1:26–36
Meditation:_____	Application: _____
_____	_____
_____	_____
_____	_____
Tuesday. Mark 6:21–44	Psalm 145:1–7, 13–17; 69:30–34; 107:8–9
Meditation:_____	Application: _____
_____	_____
_____	_____
_____	_____
Wednesday. Mark 6:45–7:13	Psalm 78:10–16, 32–39
Meditation:_____	Application: _____
_____	_____
_____	_____
_____	_____

Thursday. Mark 7:14–37

Proverbs: 6:12–19; Isaiah 59:2–3; Jeremiah 4:14; 17:9

Meditation:—————————

Application: —————————

———————————————

———————————————

———————————————

———————————————

———————————————

———————————————

Friday. Mark 8:1–26

Psalm 78:40–55

Meditation:—————————

Application: —————————

———————————————

———————————————

———————————————

———————————————

———————————————

———————————————

Weekend. Mark 8:27–9:13

Ecclesiastes 2:10–11; 12:13–14; 1 Samuel 16:6–7; 7:3–4

Meditation:—————————

Application: —————————

———————————————

———————————————

———————————————

———————————————

———————————————

———————————————

MEMORY VERSE: For what will it profit a man if he gains the whole world, and loses his own soul? Mark 8:36

DEVOTIONAL: The hardest lesson we have to learn is to trust God. The father of the demon-possessed young man had to cry for Jesus to help his unbelief (Mark 9:24). It takes the implicit faith of a child to be saved (Mark 10:15). The human tendency is to trust in ourselves, in our own means (Mark 10:24) — it takes God's grace to trust God instead (Mark 10:27), to see ourselves as servants and not masters (Mark 10:45). A servant of God who prays and trusts God to answer is the one who receives God's blessing (Mark 11:23). Jesus' enemies trusted in their own traditions, but erred out of ignorance of the Scriptures (Mark 12:24). In what, or whom, do we trust?

New Testament	Old Testament
Monday. Mark 9:14–37	Exodus 33:7–11; Job 33:31–33; Micah 4:1–2
Meditation:_____	Application: _____
_____	_____
_____	_____
_____	_____
Tuesday. Mark 9:38–10:16	Genesis 39:6–12; 2 Chronicles 15:12–16
Meditation:_____	Application: _____
_____	_____
_____	_____
_____	_____
Wednesday. Mark 10:17–41	Psalm 58:11; 73:24–26; Isaiah 58:11, 13–14
Meditation:_____	Application: _____
_____	_____
_____	_____
_____	_____

Thursday. Mark 10:42–11:14

Genesis 22:1–2, 10–12; 24:35;
26:3–5, 23–25

Meditation:_____

Application: _____

_____

_____

_____

_____

_____

_____

Friday. Mark 11:15–12:12

Joshua 10:12–14; Psalm 145:18–19

Meditation:_____

Application: _____

_____

_____

_____

_____

_____

_____

Weekend. Mark 12:13–31

Proverbs 28:10; Psalm 140:1–8;
7:1–2, 14–17; 64:2–5

Meditation:_____

Application: _____

_____

_____

_____

_____

_____

_____

MEMORY VERSE: Assuredly, I say to you, whoever does not receive the kingdom of God as a little child will by no means enter it. Mark 10:15

DEVOTIONAL: As the end approached, Jesus tried to prepare His disciples by warning them that they too would face trials before rulers (Mark 13:9). Projecting ahead to the end of the age, He prophesied the destruction of the present physical universe but assured them His word would never pass away (Mark 13:31). After the Last Supper (Mark 14:24), Jesus went to Gethsemane to pray, again warning His disciples to watch and pray because the flesh is weak (Mark 14:38), as Peter later discovered (Mark 14:72). The mistreatment Jesus prophesied in His own case came true (Mark 15:16–20). God's Word is true.

New Testament	Old Testament
Monday. Mark 12:32–13:10	Malachi 3:8–12; Exodus 35:4–9; 36:3–7
Meditation:_____	Application: _____
Tuesday. Mark 13:11–37	Daniel 11:33–35; 9:26–27; Psalm 11
Meditation:_____	Application: _____
Wednesday. Mark 14:1–26	Exodus 12:1–12
Meditation:_____	Application: _____

Thursday. Mark 14:27–52

1 Kings 8:54–59; Daniel 6:10;
Ezra 9:1–5

Meditation:_____

Application: _____

_____

_____

_____

_____

_____

_____

Friday. Mark 14:53–15:5

Psalm 27:1–4; 26:1–6

Meditation:_____

Application: _____

_____

_____

_____

_____

_____

_____

Weekend. Mark 15:6–32

Psalm 22:16–31

Meditation:_____

Application: _____

_____

_____

_____

_____

_____

_____

MEMORY VERSE: Heaven and earth will pass away, but My words will by no means pass away. Mark 13:31

DEVOTIONAL: Whether one looks at the cross (Mark 15:39) and resurrection (Mark 16:9) at the end of the Lord's life or at the angel's announcement of the Virgin Birth to Mary (Luke 1:35) at the beginning of Jesus' life; whether one listens to Zachariah's prophecy about a visitation from on high (Luke 1:78) or the angel's announcement to the shepherds of the birth of the Savior (Luke 2:11), one thing is perfectly clear: Jesus Christ is the eternal Son of God and our Savior! He was certainly conscious of who He was, even as a boy (Luke 2:49). Are we conscious of God's will in our lives?

New Testament	Old Testament
Monday. Mark 15:33–16:8	Psalm 69:19–21; Isaiah 35:3–10
Meditation:_____	Application: _____
_____	_____
_____	_____
_____	_____
Tuesday. Mark 16:9–Luke 1:13	Numbers 14:1–11
Meditation:_____	Application: _____
_____	_____
_____	_____
_____	_____
Wednesday. Luke 1:14–45	Judges 13:2–5, 24; Malachi 4:5–6
Meditation:_____	Application: _____
_____	_____
_____	_____
_____	_____

Thursday. Luke 1:46–79

Micah 7:18–20; Lamentations 3:21–26

Meditation:_____

_____

_____

_____

Application: _____

_____

_____

_____

Friday. Luke 1:80–2:26

Isaiah 12:2–5; Psalm 146:1–9

Meditation:_____

_____

_____

_____

Application: _____

_____

_____

_____

Weekend. Luke 2:27–52

1 Samuel 1:24–28; 3:4–10, 19–21

Meditation:_____

_____

_____

_____

Application: _____

_____

_____

_____

MEMORY VERSE: And the angel answered and said to her, "The Holy Spirit will come upon you, and the power of the Highest will overshadow you; therefore, also, that Holy One who is to be born will be called the Son of God." Luke 1:35

DEVOTIONAL: Among the unique details Luke gives us, following his account of Jesus' baptism and the witness of His cousin, John the Baptist (Luke 3:16), are Jesus' lineage on Mary's side (Luke 3:23) and Jesus' announcement of His public ministry in Nazareth (Luke 4:18). Jesus' ministry included healing, casting out demons (who acknowledged Him as Christ, Luke 4:41), and calling sinners to repentance (Luke 5:32). He declared Himself Lord of the Sabbath (Luke 6:5) and healed on the Sabbath (Luke 6:10), enraging the Jewish leaders. He spent much time in prayer, and invested Himself in the twelve He had chosen (Luke 6:12–13). In whom are we investing?

New Testament	Old Testament
Monday. Luke 3:1–22	Isaiah 40:1–10
Meditation:_____	Application: _____
_____	_____
_____	_____
_____	_____
Tuesday. Luke 3:23–38	Isaiah 11:1–5; Jeremiah 33:14–18; Zechariah 12:10
Meditation:_____	Application: _____
_____	_____
_____	_____
_____	_____
Wednesday. Luke 4:1–31	Isaiah 61:1–3
Meditation:_____	Application: _____
_____	_____
_____	_____
_____	_____

Thursday. Luke 4:32–5:11

2 Kings 5:1, 5–10, 13–14

Meditation:_____

Application: _____

_____

_____

_____

_____

_____

_____

Friday. Luke 5:12–35

Psalm 5:3–10; 119:145–151

Meditation:_____

Application: _____

_____

_____

_____

_____

_____

_____

Weekend. Luke 5:36–6:23

Psalm 37:7–13; 17:6–9

Meditation:_____

Application: _____

_____

_____

_____

_____

_____

_____

MEMORY VERSES: The Spirit of the LORD is upon Me, because He has anointed Me to preach the gospel to the poor; He has sent Me to heal the brokenhearted, to proclaim liberty to the captives and recovery of sight to the blind, to set at liberty those who are oppressed; to proclaim the acceptable year of the LORD Luke 4:18–19

DEVOTIONAL: Obedience to Christ's commandments is the highest priority for the Christian. Whether it is His commandment to show mercy to our enemies (Luke 6:36), or His teaching of the need to build our lives on the rock of His commandments, or His parable about the seed that fell on good ground being obedient to the Word of God (Luke 8:15), it is clear that being an obedient child of God is greater than being the greatest prophet (Luke 7:28). If only we could be as obedient to Christ as the elements are (Luke 8:25)! Obedience includes serving Christ. Jesus sent out the twelve to preach the gospel and heal the sick in His name and in His power (Luke 9:1–2). Upon their return, He took them apart for retreat (Luke 9:10). He refreshes those who serve Him.

New Testament	Old Testament
Monday. Luke 6:24–45	1 Samuel 24:7–13, 16–21
Meditation:_____	Application: _____
_____	_____
_____	_____
_____	_____
Tuesday. Luke 6:46–7:23	Psalm 18:1–5, 16–24
Meditation:_____	Application: _____
_____	_____
_____	_____
_____	_____
Wednesday. Luke 7:24–50	Proverbs 26:12; Isaiah 5:20–22; Job 11:4–6,13–17
Meditation:_____	Application: _____
_____	_____
_____	_____
_____	_____

Thursday. Luke 8:1–21

Psalm 78:1–4; Jeremiah 6:9–10; Isaiah 6:9–10

Meditation:————————

Application: ————————

————————

————————

————————

————————

————————

————————

Friday. Luke 8:22–48

Psalm 33:18–22; 9:9–11

Meditation:————————

Application: ————————

————————

————————

————————

————————

————————

————————

Weekend. Luke 8:49–9:17

2 Kings 4:42–44; Psalm 90:1–6; Job 12:7–10

Meditation:————————

Application: ————————

————————

————————

————————

————————

————————

————————

MEMORY VERSE: "Lord, Lord," and do not do the things which I say? Luke 6:46

DEVOTIONAL: What we think of Christ determines our destiny. Jesus warned against being ashamed of Him (Luke 9:26) or turning back on one's commitment to Him (Luke 9:62). Jesus is the only way to the Father (Luke 10:22); prayer to the Father must be persistent (Luke 11:9) and in Jesus' name. No wonder Jesus reacted strongly when some people attributed His miracles to the power of Satan (Luke 11:18) instead of God (Luke 11:20). For the same reason, Jesus warned against trying to please people instead of God, since God holds the keys to heaven and hell (Luke 12:5). Are we trying to please Christ?

New Testament	Old Testament
Monday. Luke 9:18–43	Nehemiah 9:25–31
Meditation:_____	Application: _____
Tuesday. Luke 9:43–10:7	2 Samuel 22:22–30; 2 Chronicles 16:7–9
Meditation:_____	Application: _____
Wednesday. Luke 10:8–29	Daniel 5:10–14; 1 Kings 4:29–34
Meditation:_____	Application: _____

Thursday. Luke 10:30–11:13

Proverbs 3:1–4, 27–28; Psalm 112:1, 4–5; Exodus 2:16–20

Meditation:_____

_____

_____

_____

_____

Application: _____

_____

_____

_____

_____

Friday. Luke 11:14–36

Proverbs 4:18–27; Numbers 15:37–41; Psalm 18:28

Meditation:_____

_____

_____

_____

_____

Application: _____

_____

_____

_____

_____

Weekend. Luke 11:37–12:7

Isaiah 51:7–8, 12–16: Proverbs 29:25; Psalm 56:3–4

Meditation:_____

_____

_____

_____

_____

Application: _____

_____

_____

_____

_____

MEMORY VERSE: So I say to you, ask, and it will be given to you; seek, and you will find; knock, and it will be opened to you. Luke 11:9

DEVOTIONAL: It takes humility to come to Christ and it takes humility to follow Christ. Failure to humble oneself and repent is to blaspheme against the Holy Spirit (Luke 12:10) and to perish forever (Luke 13:4). If we will but humble ourselves, Christ will lift us up (Luke 14:11). In the same way, if we would follow Christ as Lord we must be willing to sacrifice our own desires. Otherwise, we cannot be His disciples (Luke 14:33). The story of the prodigal [wasteful] son illustrates the need to humble ourselves and admit our spiritual bankruptcy. As soon as we take a step toward our heavenly Father, He throws His loving arms around us (Luke 15:20). Have we humbled ourselves before Him?

New Testament	Old Testament
Monday. Luke 12:8–34	Proverbs 30:7–9; 23:4–5; Ecclesiastes 5:10–11; Job 20:20–23
Meditation:_____	Application: _____
Tuesday. Luke 12:35–56	Psalm 24:1–6; Isaiah 26:7–12
Meditation:_____	Application: _____
Wednesday: Luke 12:57–13:21	Isaiah 5:1–7, 15–16
Meditation:_____	Application: _____

Thursday. Luke 13:22–14:14

Isaiah 2:12–17; Proverbs 15:33; 18:12; 3:34

Meditation:_____

Application: _____

_____

_____

_____

_____

_____

_____

Friday. Luke 14:15–15:10

Daniel 3:16–20, 26–27

Meditation:_____

Application: _____

_____

_____

_____

_____

_____

_____

Weekend. Luke 15:11–16:8

Ezekiel 33:10–15; Jeremiah 18:7–8

Meditation:_____

Application: _____

_____

_____

_____

_____

_____

_____

MEMORY VERSE: Memory Verse: Therefore you also be ready, for the Son of Man is coming at an hour you do not expect. Luke 12:40

DEVOTIONAL: Jesus prophesied His second coming in such a way that vain speculation was precluded. The clear impression from a number of illustrations is that Jesus' return will be sudden, like a flash of lightning (Luke 17:24). Until then, we are to evangelize the lost for that is why Jesus came into the world the first time (Luke 19:10). Our faithfulness in using the opportunities He gives us will be the basis of reward when He returns (Luke 19:6). The hardhearted Jewish leaders were blinded to Jesus' purposes, and to His love (Luke 19:41). Are we?

New Testament	Old Testament
Monday. Luke 16:9–17:4	Psalm 139:1–10, 13–14, 23–24
Meditation:_____	Application: _____
_____	_____
_____	_____
_____	_____
Tuesday. Luke 17:5–37	Genesis 19:1, 12–16
Meditation:_____	Application: _____
_____	_____
_____	_____
_____	_____
Wednesday. Luke 18:1–25	Jeremiah 9:23–24; Psalm 49:1–13
Meditation:_____	Application: _____
_____	_____
_____	_____
_____	_____

Thursday. Luke 18:26–19:10

Meditation:_____

_____

_____

_____

Friday. Luke 19:11–40

Meditation:_____

_____

_____

_____

Weekend. Luke 19:41–20:19

Meditation:_____

_____

_____

_____

Jonah 3:1–10; 2 Chronicles 31:1

Application: _____

_____

_____

_____

Proverbs 12:14; 24:12; Isaiah
3:10–11; Jeremiah 32:18–23

Application: _____

_____

_____

_____

Isaiah 1:10–17

Application: _____

_____

_____

_____

MEMORY VERSE: No servant can serve two masters; for either he will hate the one and love the other, or else he will be loyal to the one and despise the other. You cannot serve God and mammon. Luke 16:13

DEVOTIONAL: The governments of this world are used by Satan to oppose Christ. The Jewish leaders tried to use the paying of taxes as an issue against Jesus (Luke 20:25; 23:2). The Lord warned His disciples they would be persecuted before rulers (Luke 21:12). But God is in control; Jesus' words will not pass away (Luke 21:33). When and if we face official persecution, we must remember Jesus' willingness to die for us (Luke 22:42), His readiness to acknowledge who He was for our sake (Luke 22:70), and His promise to fill our mouth in the day of trial (Luke 21:14–15). Beyond this, we should be ready to forgive those who persecute us, as He did (Luke 23:34).

New Testament	Old Testament
Monday. Luke 20:20–47	Micah 2:1–3; Ezekiel 34:1–4, 7–10
Meditation:_____	Application: _____
_____	_____
_____	_____
_____	_____
Tuesday. Luke 21:1–28	Exodus 4:10–11, 14–16; Numbers 23:5, 7–8, 11–12
Meditation:_____	Application: _____
_____	_____
_____	_____
_____	_____
Wednesday. Luke 21:29–22:20	Psalm 119:57–60; 119:1–8; Proverbs 4:10–15; 23:19–20
Meditation:_____	Application: _____
_____	_____
_____	_____
_____	_____

Thursday. Luke 22:21–53

Meditation:_____

_____

_____

_____

Friday. Luke 22:54–23:12

Meditation:_____

_____

_____

_____

Weekend. Luke 23:13–43

Meditation:_____

_____

_____

_____

Psalm 86:1–11; 143:9–10

Application: _____

_____

_____

_____

Genesis 27:30–37, 41

Application: _____

_____

_____

_____

Isaiah 30:8–15,18; Jeremiah 36:2–3

Application: _____

_____

_____

_____

MEMORY VERSES: And He was withdrawn from them about a stone's throw, and He knelt down and prayed, saying, "Father, if it is Your will, take this cup away from Me; nevertheless not My will, but Yours, be done." Luke 22:41–42

DEVOTIONAL: Both the end of Luke and the beginning of John deal with the resurrection, the central historical fact of the Christian faith. The angels reminded the women on Easter morning that Jesus had predicted His resurrection in Galilee (Luke 24:6). Jesus showed the two men on the road to Emmaus the Bible prophecies concerning Himself (Luke 24:32). It is faith in Christ (John 1:12), the crucified "Lamb of God" (John 1:29), the One who predicted His own resurrection on His first visit to the temple (John 2:19), that saves. The one who believes in his heart that Christ has been raised from the dead is "born again" (John 3:3) and has eternal life (John 3:16). Have we received Christ by faith (John 1:12) and been born of the Spirit?

New Testament	Old Testament

Monday. Luke 23:44–24:12   Isaiah 42:1–9; 41:13–14

Meditation:_____   Application: _____

_____   _____

_____   _____

_____   _____

Tuesday. Luke 24:13–53   Deuteronomy 32:1–4; Isaiah 40:9

Meditation:_____   Application: _____

_____   _____

_____   _____

_____   _____

Wednesday. John 1:1–28   Psalm 118:22–29; Isaiah 9:2, 6; 49:5–6

Meditation:_____   Application: _____

_____   _____

_____   _____

_____   _____

Thursday. John 1:29–51

Meditation:_____

_____

_____

_____

Isaiah 53:4–12

Application: _____

_____

_____

_____

Friday. John 2:1–25

Meditation:_____

_____

_____

_____

Psalm 26:1–12; 69:6–9; 101:6–8

Application: _____

_____

_____

_____

Weekend. John 3:1–30

Meditation:_____

_____

_____

_____

Isaiah 59:12–17; 49:6

Application: _____

_____

_____

_____

MEMORY VERSE: Jesus answered and said to him, "Most assuredly, I say to you, unless one is born again, he cannot see the kingdom of God." John 3:3

DEVOTIONAL: Wherever Jesus went, He met spiritual hunger that only He could satisfy. He helped the Samaritan woman to understand spiritual worship (John 4:23); He showed His disciples the Samaritans as a field ripe for harvest (John 4:35). He met physical needs through healing, earning Him opposition (John 5:18). He multiplied the loaves and fish to feed a hungry crowd (John 6:11), but made it clear that only faith in Him satisfies the soul (John 6:35). We should understand that people will not feel their need of Christ or come to Him until the Father sovereignly takes the initiative to draw them to Himself (John 6:44, 65). Are we praying for the Holy Spirit to open the blind eyes of the lost and convict them of their need of Christ (John 6:63, 68–69)?

New Testament	Old Testament
Monday. John 3:31–4:26	Isaiah 12:1–6; Jeremiah 2:12–13, 18–19
Meditation:_____	Application: _____
_____	_____
_____	_____
_____	_____
Tuesday. John 4:27–54	2 Chronicles 20:12–17, 20–24
Meditation:_____	Application: _____
_____	_____
_____	_____
_____	_____
Wednesday. John 5:1–29	Psalm 36:1–9; 34:21–22; 27:1
Meditation:_____	Application: _____
_____	_____
_____	_____
_____	_____

Thursday. John 5:30–6:15

Deuteronomy 18:15–22;
Genesis 49:10

Meditation:_____

Application: _____

_____

_____

_____

_____

_____

_____

Friday. John 6:16–40

Psalm 66:1–7; Psalm 114:1–8;
1 Chronicles 16:8–12

Meditation:_____

Application: _____

_____

_____

_____

_____

_____

_____

Weekend. John 6:41–71

Numbers 13:17–21, 27–33

Meditation:_____

Application: _____

_____

_____

_____

_____

_____

_____

MEMORY VERSE: No one can come to Me unless the Father who sent Me draws him; and I will raise him up at the last day. John 6:44

DEVOTIONAL: The second year of Jesus' public ministry was one filled with controversy. The people were divided in their opinion of Him (John 7:12). The leaders tried to trap Him, but Jesus caused the traps to backfire, as in the case of the woman caught in adultery (John 8:7). He made astounding claims to be equal with God (John 8:58), and once again healed someone on the Sabbath (John 9:14). The former blind man's simple testimony that once he was blind and now he saw (John 9:25) enraged the leaders (John 9:28, 34), as did Jesus' indictment that it was the leaders who were blind (John 9:41). In His dialogue with the leaders, Jesus said His only purpose as the "good shepherd" was to bring life more abundant to His sheep (John 10:10), to us!

New Testament	Old Testament
Monday. John 7:1–31	Isaiah 66:2–5; 1 Kings 22:7–8
Meditation:_____	Application: _____

New Testament	Old Testament
Tuesday. John 7:32–8:11	Psalm 14:1–3; Ecclesiastes 7:20; Isaiah 64:5–7
Meditation:_____	Application: _____

New Testament	Old Testament
Wednesday. John 8:12–41	Psalm 2:2–12
Meditation:_____	Application: _____

Thursday. John 8:42–9:12   Numbers 25:1–13

Meditation:_____   Application: _____

_____   _____

_____   _____

_____   _____

Friday. John 9:13–41   Psalm 119:17–24; 146:5–10;
                                              Isaiah 42:20–21

Meditation:_____   Application: _____

_____   _____

_____   _____

_____   _____

Weekend. John 10:1–33   Psalm 23:1–6; 100; Isaiah 40:11

Meditation:_____   Application: _____

_____   _____

_____   _____

_____   _____

MEMORY VERSE: And you shall know the truth, and the truth shall make you free. John 8:32

DEVOTIONAL: The trigger that moved the Jewish leaders to act against Jesus was His raising of Lazarus from the dead (John 11:43). This stunning miracle so close to Jerusalem brought curiosity seekers to see Jesus and Lazarus (John 12:9), and crowds to hail Jesus on Palm Sunday (John 12:13). Events moved quickly after that, with Jesus warning those who did not believe of judgment to come (John 12:48). Jesus' final days were filled with teaching His disciples to serve (John 13:14) and love one another (John 13:34), with words of comfort that He would return for them (John 14:3), and with promises that He would answer their prayers (John 14:14) and send the Holy Spirit to dwell within them (John 14:17). In the meanwhile, they were (and we are) to obey Him (John 14:23).

New Testament	Old Testament
Monday. John 10:34–11:27	Psalm 40:1–5; Isaiah 25:1, 8–9
Meditation:_____	Application: _____
_____	_____
_____	_____
_____	_____
Tuesday. John 11:28–57	1 Kings 17:12–13, 15–17, 19–22, 24
Meditation:_____	Application: _____
_____	_____
_____	_____
_____	_____
Wednesday. John 12:1–26	Psalm 10:1–11, 14–16
Meditation:_____	Application: _____
_____	_____
_____	_____
_____	_____

Thursday. John 12:27–13:5   Numbers 11:10–15, 18, 21–23

Meditation:_____   Application: _____

_____   _____

_____   _____

_____   _____

Friday. John 13:6–35   Exodus 20:1–17

Meditation:_____   Application: _____

_____   _____

_____   _____

_____   _____

Weekend. John 13:36–14:26   Deuteronomy 11:1–10

Meditation:_____   Application: _____

_____   _____

_____   _____

_____   _____

MEMORY VERSES: A new commandment I give to you, that you love one another; as I have loved you, that you also love one another. By this all will know that you are My disciples, if you have love for one another. John 13:34–35

DEVOTIONAL: Our personal relationship to Jesus Christ entails total dependence on Him and on the truth of His Word (John 15:5). He promised that the Holy Spirit will guide us into all truth (John 16:13). It is through the truth of God's Word that we are sanctified (John 17:17) and that we come to believe on Christ in the first place (John 17:20). Christ came to bear witness to the truth and everyone who is of the truth, who is saved, believes the truth Christ reveals through His Word (John 18:37). When the Jewish leaders accused Jesus (correctly) of claiming to be the Son of God (John 19:7), this frightened Pilate (John 19:8) and he tried to release Jesus, finally caving in to the leaders' pressure (John 19:12). Out of spite, Pilate had a truthful sign nailed to the cross: "The King of the Jews " (John 19:19).

New Testament	Old Testament
Monday. John 14:27–15:27	Psalm 51:10–13; 33:12–22
Meditation:_____	Application: _____
_____	_____
_____	_____
_____	_____
Tuesday. John 16:1–28	Isaiah 40:27–31; Psalm 37:3–6; Proverbs 15:29
Meditation:_____	Application: _____
_____	_____
_____	_____
_____	_____
Wednesday. John 16:29–17:19	Psalm 91:1–16; Deuteronomy 33:29
Meditation:_____	Application: _____
_____	_____
_____	_____
_____	_____

Thursday. John 17:20–18:18   Psalm 133:1–3; Isaiah 66:19–23

Meditation:_____   Application: _____

_____   _____

_____   _____

_____   _____

_____

Friday. John 18:19–19:3   Psalm 117:1–2; 119:137–142;
                              33:4–5; Isaiah 45:18–19, 21

Meditation:_____   Application: _____

_____   _____

_____   _____

_____   _____

Weekend. John 19:4–27   2 Chronicles 20:5–6; Jeremiah
                              27:4–7; Daniel 4:28–32

Meditation:_____   Application: _____

_____   _____

_____   _____

_____   _____

_____   _____

MEMORY VERSE: I do not pray for these alone, but also for those who will
believe in Me through their word. John 17:20

DEVOTIONAL: Jesus died of a broken heart because of our sins, as became clear when blood and water issued from Jesus' side (John 19:34). He was buried (John 19:40–42); and He rose on the third day, appearing to ten of the apostles that evening and to Thomas eight days later (John 20:28). These facts do not exhaust the story of Jesus (John 21:25), but it was to these essential elements that they were to bear witness (Acts 1:8), which they did powerfully on Pentecost (Acts 2:4). The beginning of the church is a thrilling story: people gladly received the Word, were baptized, were instructed in doctrine, observed the Lord's Supper, met for fellowship and prayer (Acts 2:41–42), were filled with brotherly love (Acts 2:44–45) and joy (Acts 2:46), and had a wonderful testimony (Acts 2:47). Is this true of us?

New Testament	Old Testament
Monday. John 19:28–20:9	Psalm 47:1–9; Isaiah 53:10–12; Job 19:25–27
Meditation:_____	Application: _____
_____	_____
_____	_____
_____	_____
Tuesday: John 20:10–21:3	Judges 6:12–18, 36–37
Meditation:_____	Application: _____
_____	_____
_____	_____
_____	_____
Wednesday. John 21:4–25	Numbers 27:15–17; Ezekiel 34:1–6, 11, 30–31
Meditation:_____	Application: _____
_____	_____
_____	_____
_____	_____

Thursday. Acts 1:1–26

Psalm 98:1–6; 96:10–13

Meditation:_____

Application: _____

_____

_____

_____

_____

_____

_____

Friday. Acts 2:1–28

Isaiah 44:1–8

Meditation:_____

Application: _____

_____

_____

_____

_____

_____

_____

Weekend. Acts 2:29–3:10

Psalm 130:1–8; Hosea 6:1–3, 5–6

Meditation:_____

Application: _____

_____

_____

_____

_____

_____

_____

MEMORY VERSE: But you shall receive power when the Holy Spirit has come upon you; and you shall be witnesses to Me in Jerusalem, and in all Judea and Samaria, and to the end of the earth. Acts 1:8

DEVOTIONAL: The Holy Spirit turned Peter into a bold preacher who declared in his first encounter with the Jewish leaders that Jesus' name is the only one that saves (Acts 4:12). When Peter and John returned, the believers had a prayer and praise meeting that shook the place (Acts 4:31)! When the Sanhedrin arrested the apostles again, they said that they had to obey God and not man (Acts 5:29). After the deacons were ordained, God used Stephen in the same powerful way (Acts 6:10). During his trial, Stephen underscored the fact that the people of Israel rejected Moses' leadership on more than one occasion (Acts 7:27, 35, 39). He also pointed out Moses' prophecy of a Prophet to come whom the people would hear (Acts 7:37). The Holy Spirit can make us bold witnesses too!

New Testament	Old Testament
Monday. Acts 3:11–4:12	Psalm 118:19–23; Isaiah 28:14–18
Meditation:_____	Application: _____
_____	_____
_____	_____
_____	_____
Tuesday. Acts 4:13–37	Isaiah 43:1–7, 11–13
Meditation:_____	Application: _____
_____	_____
_____	_____
_____	_____
Wednesday. Acts 5:1–26	Joshua 7:20–21, 24–25; Ecclesiastes 5:2–7
Meditation:_____	Application: _____
_____	_____
_____	_____
_____	_____

Thursday. Acts 5:27–6:7

Isaiah 46:8–13; Ecclesiastes 3:14–15; Job 23:13–16

Meditation:_____

_____

_____

_____

Application: _____

_____

_____

_____

Friday. Acts 6:8–7:16

Psalm 105:1–20

Meditation:_____

_____

_____

_____

Application: _____

_____

_____

_____

Weekend. Acts 7:17–42

Psalm 105:27–45

Meditation:_____

_____

_____

_____

Application: _____

_____

_____

_____

MEMORY VERSE: Nor is there salvation in any other, for there is no other name under heaven given among men by which we must be saved. Acts 4:12

DEVOTIONAL: After the Sanhedrin stoned Stephen (Acts 7:59), another deacon, Philip, preached a revival in Samaria (Acts 8:5), leading Peter and John to come up. When Simon the sorcerer tried to buy the power to make the Holy Spirit fall, Peter rebuked him (Acts 8:20). Not long after, Saul of Tarsus was on his way to Damascus to persecute the church, when he met Jesus (Acts 9:5). After his conversion, Saul came to Jerusalem to join the disciples. He was befriended by Barnabas who introduced him to the apostles (Acts 9:27). Later, Peter had a vision in Joppa to prepare him for his first mission to the Gentiles (Acts 10:15). When he preached Jesus to the household of the Roman Centurion, Cornelius, and saw the Holy Spirit fall, it became clear to him that God had granted repentance to the Gentiles also (Acts 10:45). The gospel is for everyone!

New Testament	Old Testament

Monday. Acts 7:42–8:1

2 Chronicles 24:18–22; 36:12–17

Meditation:_____

Application: _____

_____

_____

_____

_____

_____

_____

Tuesday. Acts 8:2–25

Numbers 16:1–3, 8–11, 28–35

Meditation:_____

Application: _____

_____

_____

_____

_____

_____

_____

Wednesday. Acts 8:26–9:9
Meditation:_____

Nehemiah 8:4–12
Application: _____

_____

_____

_____

_____

_____

_____

Thursday. Acts 9:10–35

1 Samuel 16:1–7, 11–12

Meditation:_____

Application: _____

_____

_____

_____

_____

_____

_____

Friday. Acts 9:36–10:23

Psalm 25:2–7; 1 Kings 9:1–3

Meditation:_____

Application: _____

_____

_____

_____

_____

_____

_____

Weekend. Acts 10:23–48

Isaiah 1:18–20; 55:7; Psalm
65:1–4, 11–13; Exodus 34:6–7

Meditation:_____

Application: _____

_____

_____

_____

_____

_____

_____

_____

_____

MEMORY VERSE: And those of the circumcision who believed were astonished, as many as came with Peter, because the gift of the Holy Spirit had been poured out on the Gentiles also. Acts 10:45

DEVOTIONAL: Just as the Holy Spirit prompted the local church at Antioch to commission Paul and Barnabas to go on the first missionary journey (Acts 13:2), so He is giving a new burst of missionary vision to local churches today, with many young people and adults answering the call to go on short-term mission trips. God's calling to help fulfill the Great Commission is not restricted to career missionaries, but is extended to each one of us. Are we listening?

New Testament	Old Testament
Monday. Acts 11:1–30	Deuteronomy 15:4–10
Meditation:_____	Application: _____
_____	_____
_____	_____
_____	_____
Tuesday. Acts 12:1–25	Exodus 14:15–22, 31
Meditation:_____	Application: _____
_____	_____
_____	_____
_____	_____
Wednesday. Acts 13:1–25	Psalm 106:7–12; Exodus 4:31; 2 Kings 5:14–17
Meditation:_____	Application: _____
_____	_____
_____	_____
_____	_____

Thursday. Acts 13:26–52

Psalm 92:1–8; 30:4–5, 11–12; Jeremiah 15:16

Meditation:—————————

Application: —————————

—————————————

—————————————

—————————————

—————————————

—————————————

—————————————

Friday. Acts 14:1–28

1 Chronicles 14:9–14, 16–17; Proverbs 3:5–7

Meditation:—————————

Application: —————————

—————————————

—————————————

—————————————

—————————————

—————————————

—————————————

Weekend. Acts 15:1–21

Psalm 67:1–5; 22:27–28; Isaiah 45:22; 56:8

Meditation:—————————

Application: —————————

—————————————

—————————————

—————————————

—————————————

—————————————

—————————————

MEMORY VERSE: But we believe that through the grace of the Lord Jesus Christ we shall be saved in the same manner as they. Acts 15:11

DEVOTIONAL: The apostle Paul was a pioneer missionary at heart (see Romans 15:20–24). Because he was, Europe was opened up for the gospel. As a result of his second missionary journey, the gospel reached us some nineteen plus centuries later. With the knowledge that there are still thousands of people groups in the world today who do not have even one portion of Scripture in their own language, what should the emphasis of the church's missions programs be?

New Testament	Old Testament
Monday. Acts 15:22–16:10	Proverbs 25:11; Ruth 2:8–12
Meditation:_____	Application: _____
Tuesday. Acts 16:11–34	Genesis 18:1–8; 2 Kings 4:8–10; Judges 19:20–21
Meditation:_____	Application: _____
Wednesday. Acts 16:35–17:15	Isaiah 55:10–11; Psalm 119:105–108; Deuteronomy 31:24–29
Meditation:_____	Application: _____

Thursday. Acts 17:16–18:4

Genesis 2:4–7; Job 38:1, 4–7, 22–25, 36; Job 40:12, 14

Meditation:_____

_____

_____

_____

Application: _____

_____

_____

_____

Friday. Acts 18:5–28

Psalm 121:5–8; Psalm 46:1–3, 7; Deuteronomy 7:17–21

Meditation:_____

_____

_____

_____

Application: _____

_____

_____

_____

Weekend. Acts 19:1–22

2 Kings 11:17–18; Deuteronomy 17:17–19; 2 Chronicles 34:1–7

Meditation:_____

_____

_____

_____

_____

Application: _____

_____

_____

_____

_____

MEMORY VERSES: For as I was passing through and considering the objects of your worship, I even found an altar with this inscription: TO THE UNKNOWN GOD. Therefore, the One whom you worship without knowing, Him I proclaim to you. Acts 17:23

DEVOTIONAL: Paul's devotion to the Lord Jesus Christ and to the ministry of the gospel gave him a holy boldness, even as he returned to Jerusalem at the end of his third missionary journey with the knowledge that "chains and tribulations" awaited him (Acts 20:23). We do not know what price we may have to pay for standing up for our faith, but we do have the promise of the Lord Himself that He will never leave us nor forsake us (Matthew 28:20; Hebrews 13:5), a promise He kept to Paul (Acts 23:11).

New Testament	Old Testament
Monday. Acts 19:23–20:6	Psalm 124:1–8; Nehemiah 4:7–9, 14–15
Meditation:_____	Application: _____
_____	_____
_____	_____
_____	_____
Tuesday. Acts 20:7–38	1 Kings 19:4–10
Meditation:_____	Application: _____
_____	_____
_____	_____
_____	_____
Wednesday. Acts 21:1–25	Exodus 32:1–4, 26–29
Meditation:_____	Application: _____
_____	_____
_____	_____
_____	_____

Thursday. Acts 21:26–22:5

Ezekiel 2:1–7; 3:4–11

Meditation:_____

Application: _____

_____

_____

_____

_____

_____

_____

Friday. Acts 22:6–29

Psalm 33:6–12; Jeremiah 29:11–13; Isaiah 22:9–12

Meditation:_____

Application: _____

_____

_____

_____

_____

_____

_____

Weekend. Acts 22:30–23:22

Psalm 75:1–10; Psalm 92:12–15

Meditation:_____

Application: _____

_____

_____

_____

_____

_____

_____

MEMORY VERSE: But the following night the Lord stood by him and said, "Be of good cheer, Paul; for as you have testified for Me in Jerusalem so you must also bear witness at Rome." Acts 23:11

DEVOTIONAL: Paul's chief defense against his accusers was the purity of his life, his uprightness before the Law of God and the law of man (Acts 25:8; 26:4–5). This forced his enemies to trump up charges they could not prove, and led the Roman governor and King Agrippa to conclude he had done nothing worthy of death or imprisonment (Acts 26:31). Had he not appealed to Caesar, he might have been set free (Acts 26:32). If we were charged with being a Christian, would there be enough evidence to convict us?

New Testament	Old Testament
Monday. Acts 23:23–24:16	2 Chronicles 31:20–21; 2 Kings 18:5–6; 2 Chronicles 17:3–6
Meditation _____	Application: _____
_____	_____
_____	_____
_____	_____
Tuesday. Acts 24:17–25:12	Genesis 3:7–10; Nahum 1:2, 6; Ezekiel 21:1–6
Meditation:_____	Application: _____
_____	_____
_____	_____
_____	_____
Wednesday. Acts 25:13–26:8	2 Samuel 22:21–25; Psalm 37:17–19, 30–33, 39–40; Job 2:3
Meditation:_____	Application: _____
_____	_____
_____	_____
_____	_____

Thursday. Acts 26:9–32

Exodus 15:11–14; Deuteronomy
4:5–7; 2 Samuel 7:18–22

Meditation:_____

Application: _____

_____

_____

_____

_____

_____

_____

Friday. Acts 27:1–26

Joshua 1:1–9; 1 Kings 8:56

Meditation:_____

Application: _____

_____

_____

_____

_____

_____

_____

Weekend. Acts 27:27–28:10

Psalm 107:23–30; Jonah 1:4–5,
12, 15–16

Meditation:_____

Application: _____

_____

_____

_____

_____

_____

_____

MEMORY VERSE: Then Agrippa said to Paul, "You almost persuade me to become a Christian." Acts 26:28

DEVOTIONAL: The banner cry of the Reformation was "justification by faith." Paul was writing in Romans to both Jewish and gentile Christians to clarify the basis of their salvation. The righteousness we need to enter heaven is not our own, but Christ's. We have His perfect character and merit credited to us by faith, by believing in and receiving the benefit of His atoning death on the cross and of His resurrection from the dead. All of this is ours when we receive Jesus Christ as Savior and Lord.

New Testament	Old Testament
Monday. Acts 28:11–31	Genesis 24:17–33
Meditation:_____	Application: _____
_____	_____
_____	_____
_____	_____
Tuesday. Romans 1:1–27	Psalm 19:1–4; 119:89–91; 97:1–6
Meditation:_____	Application: _____
_____	_____
_____	_____
_____	_____
Wednesday. Romans 1:28–2:16	Psalm 94:1–15; Proverbs 5:21–23; 15:9–11
Meditation:_____	Application: _____
_____	_____
_____	_____
_____	_____

Thursday. Romans 2:17–3:18

Meditation:_____

_____

_____

_____

Friday. Romans 3:19–4:12

Meditation:_____

_____

_____

_____

Weekend. Romans 4:13–5:11

Meditation:_____

_____

_____

_____

_____

Jeremiah 7:3, 5–7; Micah 3:8–12

Application: _____

_____

_____

_____

Genesis 15:1–6; Psalm 20:6–8;
32:10–11; 147:10–11

Application: _____

_____

_____

_____

Psalm 69:13; 62:5–6;
Isaiah 63:7–9; 48:10–11; 38:15–17

Application: _____

_____

_____

_____

_____

MEMORY VERSES: For I am not ashamed of the gospel of Christ, for it is the power of God to salvation for everyone who believes, for the Jew first and also for the Greek. For in it the righteousness of God is revealed from faith to faith; as it is written, "The just shall live by faith." Romans 1:16–17

DEVOTIONAL: Once we receive Christ's righteousness—His life; by faith, we have eternal life. But this eternal life is not just an eternal extension of this life; it is a brand new life, and a new lifestyle. We have Christ living in us when the Holy Spirit enters our hearts upon receiving Christ by faith as Savior and Lord (Romans 8:9). The presence of the Holy Spirit gives us new life in Christ, and a new power for living in accordance with God's righteous commandments (Romans 8:4).

New Testament	Old Testament
Monday. Romans 5:12–6:14	Isaiah 1:4; Jeremiah 3:19–23; 18:11–12
Meditation:_____	Application: _____
Tuesday. Romans 6:15–7:13	Psalm 95:6–7; Deuteronomy 7:6–8; 10:12, 20–21
Meditation:_____	Application: _____
Wednesday. Romans 7:14–8:17	Joshua 24:1, 14–18, 25–26
Meditation:_____	Application: _____

Thursday. Romans 8:18–39

Isaiah 59:12–17, 21; Psalm 136:1–3, 23–25

Meditation:_____

Application: _____

_____

_____

_____

_____

_____

_____

Friday. Romans 9:1–29

Isaiah 45:6–7, 9; Job 40:1–8

Meditation:_____

Application: _____

_____

_____

_____

_____

_____

_____

Weekend. Romans 9:30–10:21

Leviticus 18:1–5; Deuteronomy 30:11–14; Psalm 19:1–4

Meditation:_____

Application: _____

_____

_____

_____

_____

_____

_____

MEMORY VERSE: There is therefore now no condemnation to those who are in Christ Jesus, who do not walk according to the flesh, but according to the Spirit. Romans 8:1

DEVOTIONAL: In reading all of Paul's letters, it is clear that he bases his admonitions for Christian living on the truth of Christian doctrine. Conversely, doctrinal truth always has practical implications. Those who are forgiven based on faith in the work of Christ need to forgive others (see Romans 14:10). If Christ loved us, we need to love one another (see Romans 13:8–10). Being a child of God impacts absolutely every relationship we have.

New Testament	Old Testament
Monday. Romans 11:1–21	Ezekiel 18:21–23; Psalm 85:7–13; Isaiah 45:22–24
Meditation:_____	Application: _____
_____	_____
_____	_____
_____	_____
Tuesday. Romans 11:22–12:8	1 Samuel 15:13–23
Meditation:_____	Application: _____
_____	_____
_____	_____
_____	_____
Wednesday. Romans 12:9–13:14	Psalm 37:21, 26; 112:4–9; Proverbs 22:7; 6:1–5
Meditation:_____	Application: _____
_____	_____
_____	_____
_____	_____

Thursday. Romans 14:1–15:3

Ecclesiastes 12:13–14; Isaiah 43: 6–7; Ezekiel 36:21–23, 26–27

Meditation:_____

Application: _____

_____

_____

_____

_____

_____

_____

Friday. Romans 15:4–29

Psalm 33:18–22; 119:49–50; 29:11; Lamentations 3:21–25

Meditation:_____

Application: _____

_____

_____

_____

_____

_____

_____

Weekend. Romans 15:30–16:27

Deuteronomy 13:4–10; Ezekiel 13:3, 7

Meditation:_____

Application: _____

_____

_____

_____

_____

_____

_____

_____

_____

MEMORY VERSES: I beseech you therefore, brethren, by the mercies of God, that you present your bodies a living sacrifice, holy, acceptable to God, which is your reasonable service. And do not be conformed to this world, but be transformed by the renewing of your mind, that you may prove what is that good and acceptable and perfect will of God. Romans 12:1–2

DEVOTIONAL: Corinth had the reputation of being a fleshly city, and the church there imbibed the ways of the world. There was divisiveness, intellectual pride, and sexual immorality — all problems in the church today as much as then. Paul had to get down to the basics of the Christian life and the Christian message because of the immaturity of the Corinthians. He would like to have led them into the deeper things of Christ, but first they had to master the basics. So must we.

New Testament	Old Testament
Monday. 1 Corinthians 1:1–25	Job 12:12–13, 16–25; Isaiah 44:24–26
Meditation:_____	Application: _____
Tuesday. 1 Corinthians 1:26–2:16	Job 28:13–28
Meditation:_____	Application: _____
Wednesday. 1 Corinthians 3:1–4:5	Psalm 118:22; Zechariah 13:8–9; 10:2–6
Meditation:_____	Application: _____

Thursday. 1 Corinthians 4:6–5:8

Deuteronomy 17:2–7, 12–13;
Isaiah 1:24–28

Meditation:_____

Application: _____

_____

_____

_____

_____

_____

_____

Friday. 1 Corinthians 5:9–6:20

Numbers 25:1–3, 6–13; Proverbs
6:27–29

Meditation:_____

Application: _____

_____

_____

_____

_____

_____

_____

Weekend. 1 Corinthians 7:1–24

Proverbs 18:22; Malachi 2:13–16;
Genesis 24:1–8

Meditation:_____

Application: _____

_____

_____

_____

_____

_____

_____

MEMORY VERSE: But the natural man does not receive the things of the Spirit of God, for they are foolishness to him; nor can he know them, because they are spiritually discerned. 1 Corinthians 2:14

DEVOTIONAL: Some of the basics dealt with by Paul included marriage and divorce, Christian liberty and the body of Christ, authority in the church and home, gifts of the Spirit and the love which Christ gives. In the end, if the Holy Spirit controls my life, I can deal with temptation and demonstrate the love of Christ toward others. If self is on the throne of my life, I will seek to gratify my own desires at the expense of others.

New Testament	Old Testament
Monday. 1 Corinthians 7:25–8:8	Jeremiah 1:4–10; 16:1–2; Deuteronomy 17:14–15, 17
Meditation:_____	Application: _____
_____	_____
_____	_____
_____	_____
Tuesday. 1 Corinthians 8:9–9:18	Amos 2:11–16; Numbers 6:1–8; Malachi 2:7–8
Meditation:_____	Application: _____
_____	_____
_____	_____
_____	_____
Wednesday. 1 Corinthians 9:19–10:22	Genesis 3:1–6; Job 2:3, 6–7, 9–10
Meditation:_____	Application: _____
_____	_____
_____	_____
_____	_____
_____	_____

Thursday. 1 Corinthians 10:23–11:22   1 Samuel 2:12, 17, 22–25, 29–31

Meditation:_____   Application: _____

_____   _____

_____   _____

_____   _____

Friday. 1 Corinthians 11:23–12:13   Deuteronomy 34:9; Isaiah
11:1–2; Numbers 11:24–25

Meditation:_____   Application: _____

_____   _____

_____   _____

_____   _____

Weekend. 1 Corinthians 12:14–   Ruth 2:14–20
13:13
Meditation:_____   Application: _____

_____   _____

_____   _____

_____   _____

MEMORY VERSE: No temptation has overtaken you except such as is common to man; but God is faithful, who will not allow you to be tempted beyond what you are able, but with the temptation will also make the way of escape, that you may be able to bear it. 1 Corinthians 10:13

DEVOTIONAL: Paul taught orderliness in church worship and the exercise of spiritual gifts. He also made clear what is the heart of the gospel (1 Corinthians 15:3–4), including Christ's resurrection. Paul underscores the serious consequences of denying the bodily resurrection of Jesus Christ, and then affirms His resurrection (and ours). He encourages us by telling us that our service for Christ is not in vain (1 Corinthians 15:58), and teaches us about systematic giving in the church. Paul had a pastor's heart and grounded the churches he established in solid Christian doctrine. Our pulpits and Sunday school classes must do the same.

New Testament	Old Testament
Monday. 1 Corinthians 14:1–25	1 Kings 13:1–3; 2 Kings 23:13–16
Meditation:_____	Application: _____
_____	_____
_____	_____
_____	_____
Tuesday. 1 Corinthians 14:26–15:11	Isaiah 53:4–10; Psalm 47:5–8
Meditation:_____	Application: _____
_____	_____
_____	_____
_____	_____
Wednesday. 1 Corinthians 15:12–44	Isaiah 25:6–8; Daniel 12:1–3; Psalm 49:13–15
Meditation:_____	Application: _____
_____	_____
_____	_____
_____	_____

Thursday. 1 Corinthians 15:44–16:24

Jeremiah 18:18; Psalm 35:1, 7–8

Meditation:_____

Application: _____

_____

_____

_____

_____

_____

_____

Friday. 2 Corinthians 1:1–17

Psalm 56:1–4; Psalm 119:64–80

Meditation:_____

Application: _____

_____

_____

_____

_____

_____

_____

Weekend. 2 Corinthians 1:18–3:3

Genesis 50:15–21; Psalm 32:1–6

Meditation:_____

Application: _____

_____

_____

_____

_____

_____

_____

MEMORY VERSE: Therefore, my beloved brethren, be steadfast, immovable, always abounding in the work of the Lord, knowing that your labor is not in vain in the Lord. 1 Corinthians 15:58

DEVOTIONAL: The greatest harm to the witness of the church of the Lord Jesus Christ in our day has been the spectacle of professing Christian leaders who have been led astray into impurity and thereby have given occasion to the enemies of the gospel to ridicule the cause of Christ. Paul had to plead with the Corinthians to maintain their purity in a dark and sinful world, to separate themselves from the fleshly society in which they lived. So must we!

New Testament	Old Testament
Monday. 2 Corinthians 3:4–4:15	Isaiah 5:11–12; Proverbs 4:18–19; Job 24:12–13, 24
Meditation:_____	Application: _____
Tuesday. 2 Corinthians 4:16–6:2	Psalm 24:3–10; Isaiah 60:1, 18–20
Meditation:_____	Application: _____
Wednesday. 2 Corinthians 6:3–7:7	Psalm 119:1–3, 9–11; 18:25–26; Deuteronomy 7:1–4; Proverbs 4:14–15
Meditation:_____	Application: _____

Thursday. 2 Corinthians 7:8–8:15

Ezra 10:1–5, 10–11, 14–16

Meditation:_____

Application: _____

_____

_____

_____

_____

_____

_____

Friday. 2 Corinthians 8:16–9:15

Deuteronomy 14:22–29; Proverbs 28:27; 21:25–26

Meditation:_____

Application: _____

_____

_____

_____

_____

_____

_____

Weekend. 2 Corinthians 10:1–11:4

Jeremiah 23:25–29; 2 Chronicles 20:20–22; Psalm 55:16–19

Meditation:_____

Application: _____

_____

_____

_____

_____

_____

_____

MEMORY VERSE: Therefore, if anyone is in Christ, he is a new creation; old things have passed away; behold, all things have become new.
2 Corinthians 5:17

DEVOTIONAL: Galatians is nothing if it is not a letter setting forth the grace of God as the basis of our salvation. The law convicts all of us as sinners and we stand condemned under the law. The glorious gospel of God's free gift of grace, His unmerited favor in granting us forgiveness for all of our sins based on faith in Christ's crucifixion and resurrection on our behalf, has set us free from our sentence of spiritual death and granted us eternal life!

New Testament	Old Testament
Monday. 2 Corinthians 11:5–33	Exodus 1:11–14, 22; 2:1–3, 5, 7–10
Meditation:_____	Application: _____
_____	_____
_____	_____
_____	_____
Tuesday. 2 Corinthians 12:1–13:4	Exodus 14:13–14; 1 Samuel 30:1–4, 7–8
Meditation _____	Application: _____
_____	_____
_____	_____
_____	_____
Wednesday. 2 Corinthians 13:5 Galatians 1:20	1 Chronicles 17:7–9, 11; 1 Samuel 9:14–17
Meditation:_____	Application: _____
_____	_____
_____	_____
_____	_____
_____	_____

Thursday. Galatians 1:21–2:21
113:5–8;

Nehemiah 8:9–10; Psalm
Leviticus 25:35–38

Meditation:_____

Application: _____

_____

_____

_____

_____

_____

_____

Friday. Galatians 3:1–20

Genesis 22:15–18; 1 Kings 2:1–4;
Psalm 18:30–36

Meditation:_____

Application: _____

_____

_____

_____

_____

_____

_____

Weekend. Galatians 3:21–4:20

Isaiah 64:8–9; Hosea 1:10–11;
Deuteronomy 14:2; 32:3, 5–10

Meditation:_____

Application: _____

_____

_____

_____

_____

_____

_____

Memory Verse: I have been crucified with Christ; it is no longer I who live, but Christ lives in me; and the life which I now live in the flesh I live by faith in the Son of God, who loved me and gave Himself for me. Galatians 2:20

DEVOTIONAL: Paul plead with the Ephesians to strive to keep the unity produced by the Spirit as He binds us together with His peace (Ephesians 4:3). We believers form the body of Christ (Ephesians 4:12), and we need each other — we need the gifts of grace God has distributed among us for the purpose of building up one another (Ephesians 4:16). No believer is an island; God has attached us to one another for the work of the ministry. Let us reach out to fellow believers with arms of love, just as He loves us.

New Testament

Old Testament

Monday. Galatians 4:21–5:15

Genesis 15:1–4; 16:1–4; 21:8–12

Meditation:_____

Application: _____

_____

_____

_____

_____

_____

_____

Tuesday. Galatians 5:16–6:18

Ecclesiastes 2:26; Proverbs 3:3–4; 23:29–32; Psalm 37:7–9

Meditation:_____

Application: _____

_____

_____

_____

_____

_____

_____

Wednesday. Ephesians 1:1–2:3

Daniel 2:14–18; Job 42:7–9; Deuteronomy 9:18

Meditation:_____

Application: _____

_____

_____

_____

_____

_____

_____

Thursday. Ephesians 2:4–3:6

Isaiah 57:16–19; Micah 7:18–19;
Daniel 9:17–18; Psalm 86:12–13

Meditation:_____

Application: _____

_____

_____

_____

_____

_____

_____

_____

_____

Friday. Ephesians 3:7–4:16

1 Chronicles 16:28–29, 34;
16:39–41; Psalm 136:1, 4–9, 26

Meditation:_____

Application: _____

_____

_____

_____

_____

_____

_____

_____

_____

Weekend. Ephesians 4:17–5:14

Proverbs 1:10, 15–19; 28:20;
30:15–16; Jeremiah 8:10–12

Meditation:_____

Application: _____

_____

_____

_____

_____

_____

_____

_____

_____

MEMORY VERSES: For by grace you have been saved through faith, and that not of yourselves; it is the gift of God, not of works, lest anyone should boast. Ephesians 2:8–9

DEVOTIONAL: In Philippians, Paul exhorts the church to have the attitude of humility demonstrated by Christ (Philippians 2:5–8). Throughout the letter, he exudes joy and encourages the Philippians to rejoice in the Lord (Philippians 1:25–26; 2:17–18; 3:1, 3; 4:4, 10). The secret to having the peace and joy of the Lord is to bring everything to the Lord in prayer (Philippians 4:6), to focus our thinking exclusively on those things that flow from the mind and character of God Himself (Philippians 4:8), and to live and practice what God's Word teaches (Philippians 4:9).

New Testament	Old Testament
Monday. Ephesians 5:15–6:4	Proverbs 5:18–20; Genesis 24:34–40, 50–51, 62–67
Meditation:_____	Application: _____
Tuesday. Ephesians 6:5–24	Job 1:6–10; Daniel 10:4–7, 12–13; Psalm 106:34–37
Meditation:_____	Application: _____
Wednesday. Philippians 1:1–2:4	Proverbs 22:4; 27:2; 1 Samuel 18:17–19; Micah 6:8
Meditation:_____	Application: _____

Thursday. Philippians 2:5–30

Psalm 34:12–14; 78:17–21;
Proverbs 20:3; 16:24; 11:12

Meditation:_____

Application: _____

_____

_____

_____

_____

_____

_____

Friday. Philippians 3:1–21

Psalm 42:1–2; 63:1–8; 119:166–
173; 73:24–26

Meditation:_____

Application: _____

_____

_____

_____

_____

_____

_____

Weekend. Philippians 4:1–23

Psalm 55:22; 105:1–4; 37:3–5;
97:10–12; 68:1–3, 19–20

Meditation:_____

Application: _____

_____

_____

_____

_____

_____

_____

_____

_____

MEMORY VERSE: Finally, brethren, whatever things are true, whatever
things are noble, whatever things are just, whatever things are pure, whatever things are lovely, whatever things are of good report, if there is any virtue
and if there is anything praiseworthy—meditate on these things.
Philippians 4:8

DEVOTIONAL: Paul battled an early heresy in the Colossian church that has come back to haunt us in a new form as the New Age movement. Jewish Gnostics bought into the Greek philosophy of their day that put down the physical and glorified the spiritual, or immaterial. Specifically, these Gnostics claimed to have mystical experiences and contacts with a whole hierarchy of angelic beings descending from pure spirit, worshiping these angels. Christ is above all created spirit beings; He is equal with God as the Creator (Colossians 1:16) and has an exclusive position as our Savior. He left heaven to dwell in a body, and, through the Spirit, in us (Colossians 1:27)!

	New Testament	Old Testament

New Testament

Monday. Colossians 1:1–23

Meditation:_____
_____
_____
_____

Old Testament

Psalm 102:12, 15–22, 25–27;
Isaiah 41:2–4

Application: _____
_____
_____
_____

Tuesday. Colossians 1:24–2:15

Meditation:_____
_____
_____
_____

Psalm 40:1–4; Proverbs 4:13–15; Isaiah 50:10–11

Application: _____
_____
_____
_____

Wednesday. Colossians 2:16–3:17

Meditation:_____
_____
_____
_____

Leviticus 19:1–4, 11–18, 37;
20:7–8, 26

Application: _____
_____
_____
_____

Thursday. Colossians 3:18–4:18

Proverbs 6:20–23; 23:22–25;
Deuteronomy 21:18–21

Meditation:_____

Application: _____

_____

_____

_____

_____

_____

_____

_____

_____

Friday. 1 Thessalonians 1:1–2:16

Deuteronomy 7:6–8; Psalm 40:4–9

Meditation:_____

Application: _____

_____

_____

_____

_____

_____

_____

_____

_____

Weekend. 1 Thessalonians 2:17–
4:12

Leviticus 22:31–33; 11:44–45;
Amos 2:6–7; Psalm 99:5–9

Meditation:_____

Application: _____

_____

_____

_____

_____

_____

_____

_____

_____

MEMORY VERSE: If then you were raised with Christ, seek those things
which are above, where Christ is, sitting at the right hand of God.
Colossians 3:1

DEVOTIONAL: In both 1 Thessalonians and 2 Thessalonians, Paul clarifies issues surrounding the second coming of our Lord Jesus Christ in order to encourage and comfort the believers of Thessalonica (1 Thessalonians 4:18). They were not to be led astray by false prophecies of Christ's return (2 Thessalonians 2:2–3); not to stop working because of belief in His soon coming (2 Thessalonians 3:11–12). Instead, they (and we) are to continue obeying the Word of God (2 Thessalonians 2:15; 3:13), and so be found ready whenever He comes back.

New Testament	Old Testament
Monday. 1 Thessalonians 4:13–5:28	Job 19:25–27; Psalm 98:2–9; Isaiah 26:19
Meditation:_____	Application: _____
_____	_____
_____	_____
_____	_____
Tuesday. 2 Thessalonians 1:1–2:12	Isaiah 1:27–31; Proverbs 1:24–29
Meditation:_____	Application: _____
_____	_____
_____	_____
_____	_____
Wednesday. 2 Thessalonians 2:13–3:18	Proverbs 31:10–31; Ecclesiastes 2:26
Meditation:_____	Application: _____
_____	_____
_____	_____
_____	_____

Thursday. 1 Timothy 1:1–20

Jeremiah 33:6–9, 11; Isaiah 55:7; Psalm 103:8–14

Meditation:_____

Application: _____

_____

_____

_____

_____

_____

_____

Friday. 1 Timothy 2:1–3:13

Deuteronomy 4:34–40; Isaiah 43:10–13; 44:8

Meditation:_____

Application: _____

_____

_____

_____

_____

_____

_____

Weekend. 1 Timothy 3:14–4:16

2 Kings 22:1–2; 23:1–3, 24–25; Daniel 6:1–5

Meditation:_____

Application: _____

_____

_____

_____

_____

_____

_____

_____

_____

MEMORY VERSES: For the Lord Himself will descend from heaven with a shout, with the voice of an archangel, and with the trumpet of God. And the dead in Christ will rise first. Then we who are alive and remain shall be caught up together with them in the clouds to meet the Lord in the air. And thus we shall always be with the Lord. 1 Thessalonians 4:16–17

DEVOTIONAL: In 1 Timothy, Paul exhorts his young protégé, Timothy, to be a faithful minister, teaching the doctrine that Paul had taught him, avoiding foolish, distracting questions (1 Timothy 4:6–7). In 2 Timothy, Paul is facing execution and writes to Timothy his last charge, expressing his own confidence in God's faithfulness and power to keep him (2 Timothy 1:12). He commends Timothy to the inspired Scripture as the resource for every good work (2 Timothy 3:14–17). Paul's testimony was that he had fought a good fight, completed his work for Christ, and kept the faith (2 Timothy 4:7). May that be our life testimony as well!

New Testament	Old Testament
Monday. 1 Timothy 5:1–25	2 Samuel 12:7–9, 13–14; Leviticus 19:15–17; Proverbs 10:17, 19–21
Meditation:_____	Application: _____
_____	_____
_____	_____
_____	_____
Tuesday. 1 Timothy 6:1–21	Deuteronomy 8:11–14, 17–18; Ecclesiastes 5:10–17, 19–20
Meditation:_____	Application: _____
_____	_____
_____	_____
_____	_____
Wednesday. 2 Timothy 1:1–2:13	Deuteronomy 4:9–10; 31:9–13
Meditation:_____	Application: _____
_____	_____
_____	_____
_____	_____

Thursday. 2 Timothy 2:14–3:11

Proverbs 4:14–17, 20–27; Psalm 101:1–5

Meditation:_____

Application: _____

_____

_____

_____

_____

_____

_____

Friday. 2 Timothy 3:12–4:22

Nehemiah 8:1–3, 8, 14–18

Meditation:_____

Application: _____

_____

_____

_____

_____

_____

_____

Weekend. Titus 1:1–2:8

Isaiah 50:4–7; Leviticus 22:9; Malachi 2:5–9

Meditation:_____

Application: _____

_____

_____

_____

_____

_____

_____

_____

_____

MEMORY VERSE: For this reason I also suffer these things; nevertheless I am not ashamed, for I know whom I have believed and am persuaded that He is able to keep what I have committed to Him until that Day. 2 Timothy 1:12

DEVOTIONAL: Just as Paul taught his son in the faith, Timothy (see 1 Timothy 6:1–2), so he teaches another son in the faith, Titus (see Titus 2:9–10), that servants are to obey and honor their earthly masters. He went so far as to return a runaway slave, Onesimus (whom Paul led to Christ in Rome), to his believing master, Philemon. Paul did not make an issue of slavery, believing in the soon return of Christ (Titus 2:13). But he went a long way toward planting the seeds of Onesimus' emancipation when he urged Philemon (whom he had also led to Christ, Philemon 19) to receive his former slave not as a servant but as a beloved brother (Philemon 16). The principles of faithful service that Paul teaches apply to employee-employer relations, as part of a witness for Christ.

New Testament	Old Testament
Monday. Titus 2:9–3:15	Daniel 6:11–16, 19–23, 25–27
Meditation:_____	Application: _____
_____	_____
_____	_____
_____	_____
Tuesday. Philemon 1–25	Genesis 37:18–20, 26–28; 41:39–40, 42–43; 45:4–5, 9–11, 14–15
Meditation:_____	Application: _____
_____	_____
_____	_____
_____	_____
Wednesday. Hebrews 1:1–2:4	Exodus 15:1–3, 6–7; Psalm 86:11–13; Habakkuk 3:2–4, 12–13, 18
Meditation:_____	Application: _____
_____	_____
_____	_____
_____	_____

Thursday. Hebrews 2:5–3:6   Ezekiel 37:22–28; Isaiah 43:1, 25–28

Meditation:_____   Application: _____

_____   _____

_____   _____

_____   _____

Friday. Hebrews 3:7–4:13   Numbers 14:2–3, 6–9, 20–23;
                                               Daniel 9:2–4

Meditation:_____   Application: _____

_____   _____

_____   _____

_____   _____

Weekend. Hebrews 4:14–6:8   Genesis 14:18–20; Exodus
                                               28:1–3; Leviticus 21:10–15

Meditation:_____   Application: _____

_____   _____

_____   _____

_____   _____

MEMORY VERSES: Not by works of righteousness which we have done, but according to His mercy He saved us, through the washing of regeneration and renewing of the Holy Spirit. . . . This is a faithful saying, and these things I want you to affirm constantly, that those who have believed in God should be careful to maintain good works. These things are good and profitable to man. Titus 3:5, 8

DEVOTIONAL: Do we consider the angels, or Moses, or the high priest under the Law? Christ is superior to each one (see Hebrews 1–5). Citing the Old Testament example of Melchizedek, the priest of Salem, to whom Abraham paid tithes (making Melchizedek his superior), the writer of Hebrews says Christ our high priest is similarly superior, offering Himself once and for all as a sacrifice for our sins, establishing a new and superior covenant, and calling for us to commit ourselves to Him in faith and not draw back in unbelief (Hebrews 6–10).

New Testament	Old Testament
Monday. Hebrews 6:9–7:10	Psalm 89:20, 26–37; Joshua 23:4–6, 14–16
Meditation:_____	Application: _____
Tuesday. Hebrews 7:11–8:6	Psalm 110:1–4; Jeremiah 31:33; Ezekiel 16:59–63
Meditation:_____	Application: _____
Wednesday. Hebrews 8:7–9:12	Psalm 103:8–12; 111:7–9; Isaiah 53:10–11
Meditation:_____	Application: _____

Thursday. Hebrews 9:13–10:10

Meditation:_____

_____

_____

_____

Friday. Hebrews 10:11–39

Meditation:_____

_____

_____

_____

Weekend. Hebrews 11:1–22

Meditation:_____

_____

_____

_____

Exodus 24:3–7; Leviticus 16:15–17

Application: _____

_____

_____

_____

Isaiah 66:10, 14–16; Amos 5:4–5, 12, 14–15

Application: _____

_____

_____

_____

Genesis 15:5–6; 6:9, 11–22

Application: _____

_____

_____

_____

MEMORY VERSE: Now faith is the substance of things hoped for, the evidence of things not seen. Hebrews 11:1

DEVOTIONAL: James is very straightforward when it comes to exhorting believers to behave consistently, whether it comes to a recognition of our sinful inclinations, our lusts, our lack of prayer, our tendency to show favoritism to the well off in our congregations, or our failure to control our tongues. James exhorts us to resist the devil and humble ourselves in the sight of the Lord (James 4:7–10). He also calls on us to put our faith to work, to demonstrate our faith by lives of Christian service.

New Testament	Old Testament
Monday. Hebrews 11:23–12:6	Job 5:17–21; Psalm 119:65–72; Proverbs 3:11–12
Meditation:_____	Application: _____
Tuesday. Hebrews 12:7–29	2 Samuel 24:8–15, 17–19, 25
Meditation:_____	Application: _____
Wednesday. Hebrews 13:1–25	Deuteronomy 10:12–21; Job 31:5–6, 9–11, 16, 18–19, 24, 32
Meditation:_____	Application: _____

Thursday. James 1:1–27

1 Kings 3:4–14

Meditation:_____

Application: _____

_____

_____

_____

_____

_____

_____

Friday. James 2:1–26

Obadiah 8, 10–15; Leviticus
19:15–16

Meditation:_____

Application: _____

_____

_____

_____

_____

_____

_____

Weekend. James 3:1–4:10

Psalm 141:1–4; Proverbs 10:11,
31–32; 12:18–19; 13:3; 18:20–21

Meditation:_____

Application: _____

_____

_____

_____

_____

_____

_____

MEMORY VERSES: Thus also faith by itself, if it does not have works, is dead. But someone will say, "You have faith, and I have works." Show me your faith without your works, and I will show you my faith by my works. James 2:17–18

DEVOTIONAL: The apostle Peter wrote his first letter to churches in Asia Minor that were undergoing, or would soon undergo, severe persecution. He reminds them of their new birth by the Word, their special status as the people of God, and the privilege they have to suffer for Christ. If suffering must come, Peter is anxious that it be for the right reasons, because they are Christians, and not because of any misconduct on their part. He calls on each person to be humble under the mighty hand of God and to resist the devil, trusting God to be faithful (1 Peter 5:6–11).

New Testament	Old Testament
Monday. James 4:11–5:20	Esther 4:9–16
Meditation:_____	Application: _____
_____	_____
_____	_____
_____	_____
Tuesday. 1 Peter 1:1–21	Isaiah 48:1–2, 8, 10; Deuteronomy 8:2–3, 5; Zechariah 13:9
Meditation:_____	Application: _____
_____	_____
_____	_____
_____	_____
Wednesday. 1 Peter 1:22–2:17	Daniel 3:16–20, 26–29
Meditation:_____	Application: _____
_____	_____
_____	_____
_____	_____

Thursday. 1 Peter 2:18–3:12

Genesis 26:26–31; 1 Samuel
24:8–12; Zechariah 8:16–17, 19

Meditation:_____

Application: _____

_____

_____

_____

_____

_____

_____

Friday. 1 Peter 3:13–4:11

Psalm 31:19–20, 23–24; 62:5–8;
71:12–16; Lamentations 3:22–25

Meditation:_____

Application: _____

_____

_____

_____

_____

_____

_____

Weekend. 1 Peter 4:12–5:14

1 Kings 17:2–4, 6–16; Psalm
145:9, 13–14, 18

Meditation:_____

Application: _____

_____

_____

_____

_____

_____

_____

_____

_____

MEMORY VERSE: But sanctify the Lord God in your hearts, and always be ready to give a defense to everyone who asks you a reason for the hope that is in you, with meekness and fear. 1 Peter 3:15

DEVOTIONAL: Peter, like Paul in 2 Timothy, is aware that his own death is impending (2 Peter 1:13–15). He presents a high view of the inspiration of Scripture (2 Peter 1:19–21), warning his readers against false teachers and their immoral lifestyle (2 Peter 2). He urges them not to be impatient about Christ's second coming, attributing any delay to God's desire to extend the day of salvation (quoting Paul on this, along with other Scriptures, 2 Peter 3:15–16). Peter prophesies the consumption of the current earth and skies in fire, and the appearance of a new heaven and earth (2 Peter 3:12–13). In light of the end of the world, we should be living godly lives (2 Peter 3:11).

New Testament	Old Testament
Monday. 2 Peter 1:1–21	Proverbs 2:3–6; 1:1–5; 8:9–10; 2 Chronicles 1:7–12
Meditation:_____	Application: _____
_____	_____
_____	_____
_____	_____
Tuesday. 2 Peter 2:1–22	Isaiah 56:9–12; Hosea 4:7–10
Meditation:_____	Application: _____
_____	_____
_____	_____
_____	_____
Wednesday. 2 Peter 3:1–18	Psalm 22:3–8; Isaiah 5:18–19; Jeremiah 17:14–18
Meditation;_____	Application: _____
_____	_____
_____	_____
_____	_____

Thursday. 1 John 1:1–2:14

Isaiah 9:2; 42:6–7; Jeremiah
13:15–16; Psalm 43:3–4

Meditation:_____

Application: _____

_____

_____

_____

_____

_____

_____

Friday. 1 John 2:15–3:10
18:26–28,

Proverbs 28:13; Ezekiel
30; Ecclesiastes 2:1, 8–11

Meditation:_____

Application: _____

_____

_____

_____

_____

_____

_____

Weekend. 1 John 3:11–4:12
9:3–10

Zechariah 7:9–12; 2 Samuel

Meditation:_____

Application:_____

_____

_____

_____

_____

_____

_____

MEMORY VERSE: Therefore, since all these things will be dissolved, what manner of persons ought you to be in holy conduct and godliness . . . ? 2 Peter 3:11

DEVOTIONAL: John the Apostle's first letter focuses on those things that mark the children of God, those who are born again of His Spirit and in whom His Spirit dwells. They include a lifestyle of righteousness rather than a lifestyle of sin, a love for fellow believers, a witness for Jesus Christ as the Son of God come in the flesh. And these are interrelated. A person cannot claim to love God if he does not love his brother, or if he does not keep God's commandments. If we can affirm these marks and have Christ in us, we may know we have eternal life.

New Testament	Old Testament
Monday. 1 John 4:13–5:21	Psalm 66:16–20; Jeremiah 42:1–3, 5–6
Meditation:_____	Application: _____
Tuesday. 2 John 1–3	Deuteronomy 31:7–8; 1 Kings 2:1–4; Jeremiah 38:13, 16–18
Meditation:_____	Application: _____
Wednesday. Jude 1–13	Psalm 50:10–23; Isaiah 13:6–11
Meditation:_____	Application: _____

Thursday. Jude 14–25

Jeremiah 14:13–16; 9:23–24;
Psalm 86:4–5, 11–14, 16;
Lamentations 3:22–26

Meditation:_____

Application: _____

_____

_____

_____

_____

_____

_____

Friday. Revelation 1:1–20

Isaiah 48:12–13; 43:13; 44:6;
Psalm 41:13; 102:25–27; 90:1–4

Meditation:_____

Application: _____

_____

_____

_____

_____

_____

_____

Weekend. Revelation 2:1–17

Jeremiah 3:12; 2:1–9

Meditation:_____

Application: _____

_____

_____

_____

_____

_____

_____

MEMORY VERSE: These things I have written to you who believe in the name of the Son of God, that you may know that you have eternal life, and that you may continue to believe in the name of the Son of God. 1 John 5:13

DEVOTIONAL: The Book of the Revelation of John the Apostle is full of imagery as well as prophecy of things to come. The Lord Jesus Christ is portrayed as an awesome king sitting upon the throne of God. He is also portrayed as the Lamb who was slain and yet lives forevermore. John received messages for the seven churches of Asia Minor, some of commendation and some of warning to repent. He also saw visions of heaven, of angels, of slain martyrs, and glimpses of future tribulation as one seal after another of the scroll is opened. Our God is an awesome God!

New Testament	Old Testament
Monday. Revelation 2:18–3:6	Deuteronomy 10:12; 26:17–18, 13:1–5; 17:2, 5–7
Meditation:_____	Application: _____
_____	_____
_____	_____
_____	_____
Tuesday. Revelation 3:7–4:5	Isaiah 22:22–25; Zephaniah 1:14–16; Daniel 12:1–3
Meditation:_____	Application: _____
_____	_____
_____	_____
_____	_____
Wednesday. Revelation 4:6–6:2	Isaiah 6:1–8; Ezekiel 1:3–6
Meditation:_____	Application: _____
_____	_____
_____	_____
_____	_____

Thursday. Revelation 6:3–7:8

Nahum 1:2–6

Meditation:_____

Application: _____

_____

_____

_____

_____

_____

_____

Friday. Revelation 7:9–8:13

Isaiah 25:6–9; 51:6; 61:10

Meditation:_____

Application: _____

_____

_____

_____

_____

_____

_____

Weekend. Revelation 9:1–10:4

Joel 2:1–3, 6, 10–13

Meditation:_____

Application: _____

_____

_____

_____

_____

_____

_____

MEMORY VERSE: Behold, I stand at the door and knock. If anyone hears My voice and opens the door, I will come in to him and dine with him, and he with Me. Revelation 3:20

DEVOTIONAL: One cannot read of the three and one-half years of tribulation on the earth, or of the beast that demands worship, or of the forcing of everyone to have the mark of the beast, the number of man which is 666, without shuddering. The picture of an angry Satan, cast out of heaven onto the earth, venting his wrath because his time is short, is fearsome. But more terrible are the vials of God's wrath poured out on the unrepentant. Unsaved people should indeed fear a God of judgment, and repent while there is time.

New Testament	Old Testament
Monday. Revelation 10:5–11:14	Zechariah 4:11–14; Exodus 7:19–20; 1 Kings 17:1; 18:1–2
Meditation:_____	Application: _____
_____	_____
_____	_____
_____	_____
Tuesday. Revelation 11:15–12:12	Psalm 2:1–6; Daniel 7:13–18, 21–22
Meditation:_____	Application: _____
_____	_____
_____	_____
_____	_____
Wednesday. Revelation 12:13–13:18	Daniel 7:27; 11:29–35
Meditation:_____	Application: _____
_____	_____
_____	_____
_____	_____

Thursday. Revelation 14:1–20

Joel 3:12–13; Jeremiah 25:15–17, 26; Psalm 75:7–8

Meditation:_____

Application: _____

_____

_____

_____

_____

_____

_____

Friday. Revelation 15:1–16:11

Deuteronomy 32:1–6, 15, 19–20, 23–25

Meditation:_____

Application: _____

_____

_____

_____

_____

_____

_____

Weekend. Revelation 16:12–17:8

Ezekiel 13:8–13; 38:18–23

Meditation:_____

Application: _____

_____

_____

_____

_____

_____

_____

MEMORY VERSES: Then I saw another angel flying in the midst of heaven, having the everlasting gospel to preach to those who dwell on the earth—to every nation, tribe, tongue, and people—saying with a loud voice, "Fear God and give glory to Him, for the hour of His judgment has come; and worship Him who made heaven and earth, the sea and springs of water." Revelation 14:6–7

DEVOTIONAL: The climactic moments of human history stagger the imagination. Christ's return in power and glory with those who are His own, the seeming threat of hostile armies under the command of Satan surrounding Jerusalem, the judgment seat of Christ when the books are opened, the New Jerusalem descending out of heaven, the unrepentant enemies of Christ cast into a lake of fire to suffer separation from God forever, the redeemed reigning with Christ in glory, make us cry out with John, "Even so, come, Lord Jesus" (Revelation 22:20)!

New Testament	Old Testament
Monday. Revelation 17:9–18:10	Genesis 19:12–15; Jeremiah 51:6, 45–47
Meditation:_____	Application: _____
_____	_____
_____	_____
_____	_____
Tuesday. Revelation 18:11–24	Jeremiah 51:25–26, 36–50
Meditation:_____	Application: _____
_____	_____
_____	_____
_____	_____
Wednesday. Revelation 19:1–16	Exodus 15:11–13, 17–18; Psalm 104:31–35; 148:1–13
Meditation:_____	Application: _____
_____	_____
_____	_____
_____	_____

Thursday. Revelation 19:17–20:15

Isaiah 24:21–22; 29:6–8;
Ezekiel 39:1, 4–8

Meditation:＿＿＿＿＿＿＿

_____

_____

_____

Application: ＿＿＿＿＿＿

_____

_____

_____

Friday. Revelation 21:1–27

Isaiah 65:17–19, 22;
Zechariah 2:10–13

Meditation:＿＿＿＿＿＿＿

_____

_____

_____

Application: ＿＿＿＿＿＿

_____

_____

_____

Weekend. Revelation 22:1–21

Isaiah 55:1–3; Psalm 46:4–5a;
Ezekiel 47:1, 7–12

Meditation:＿＿＿＿＿＿＿

_____

_____

_____

_____

Application: ＿＿＿＿＿＿

_____

_____

_____

_____

MEMORY VERSE: And God will wipe away every tear from their eyes; there shall be no more death, nor sorrow, nor crying. There shall be no more pain, for the former things have passed away. Revelation 21:4